A QUICK COURSE IN

WORDPERFECT

Version 5.1

KAYE FOX

POLLY URBAN

PUBLISHED BY
Online Press Incorporated
14320 NE 21st Street, Suite 18
Bellevue, WA 98007

Publisher's Cataloging in Publication
(prepared by Quality Books Inc.)

Fox, Kaye, 1932–
    A Quick Course in WordPerfect, version 5.1 / Kaye Fox, Polly Urban.
    —

    p. cm.
    Includes index.
    ISBN 1-879399-01-6

    1. WordPerfect (Computer program) 2. Word processing.   I.
Urban, Polly, 1960–   II. Title.

Z52.5.W65   652.5'536
                                            QBI91-131
                                                          91-60294
                                                          CIP

Printed and bound in the United States of America

    3 4 5 6 7 8 9 F L O L 3 2 1 0

Distributed to bookstores by Publishers Group West, (800) 365-3453

Contents

Introduction

Learning a new word-processing program isn't easy. And it takes time—time that you probably don't have to spare. You know you'll find what you need to get started in the manual, but you'd like information that will allow you to begin generating useful documents right away. So you're now placing your bets on us and *A Quick Course in WordPerfect*.

As you know, WordPerfect is a powerful tool with a lot to offer. Presently rated #1 in word-processing software sales, it is the word processor of choice for millions of people. Our goal in this book is to show you that powerful doesn't have to mean difficult to master, and that learning to use Word-Perfect effectively can be accomplished rapidly.

What makes this book different from other WordPerfect books? First, we show you how to use WordPerfect to get your work done, not just how the program works. We walk you through the steps necessary to generate professional-looking documents. And in the process, you learn what you need to know to adapt our documents for use in your own work situation. Focusing on the features most people use most of the time, we show you step by step how to create useful memos, business letters, letterheads, and reports. In addition, we show you how to dress up your documents by importing graphics created in one of the many graphics programs now available, and how to streamline office mailings by using WordPerfect's useful Merge feature to print form documents and envelopes.

On the following pages, we supplement our instructions and discussions with handy tips and other useful items that aren't critical to the topic at hand—items that you might find interesting or helpful as you learn the program. At the beginning of each chapter, we show an example of the screen or document you will be working with and, as a memory jogger, we indicate the pages on which you will find information that you might want to look up later. Within each chapter, arrows draw your attention to procedures you might find yourself using again and again, so that they are easy to spot as you thumb through the book.

For the most part, we have followed WordPerfect's lead and stuck with the terms and conventions used in the manual. However, we have reversed WordPerfect's order in keystroke instructions, telling you, for example, to *press F10 (Save)*, instead of *press Save (F10)*. In our experience, people find it quicker and easier to memorize the keystrokes for basic procedures when instructions are presented this way.

That's about it for this introduction. Before you begin, you might want to take a moment to quickly flip through the book and see what *A Quick Course in WordPerfect* has in store for you. Then turn to Chapter 1 and jump right in.

1

First Things First

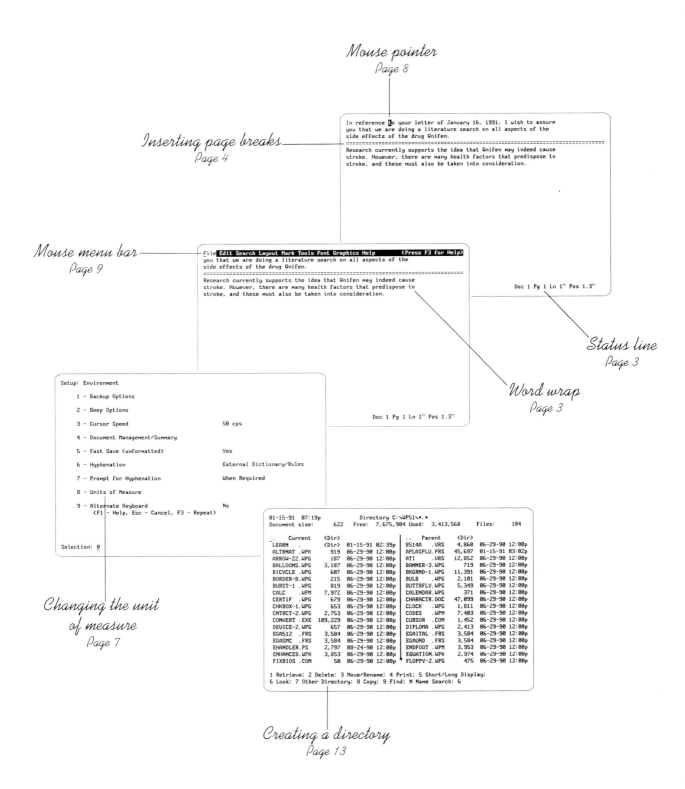

Mouse pointer
Page 8

In reference to your letter of January 16, 1991, I wish to assure
you that we are doing a literature search on all aspects of the
side effects of the drug Qnifen.
===
Research currently supports the idea that Qnifen may indeed cause
stroke. However, there are many health factors that predispose to
stroke, and these must also be taken into consideration.

Inserting page breaks
Page 4

Mouse menu bar
Page 9

File **Edit Search Layout Mark Tools Font Graphics Help   ⟨Press F3 for Help⟩**
you that we are doing a literature search on all aspects of the
side effects of the drug Qnifen.
===
Research currently supports the idea that Qnifen may indeed cause
stroke. However, there are many health factors that predispose to
stroke, and these must also be taken into consideration.

Doc 1 Pg 1 Ln 1" Pos 1.3"

Status line
Page 3

Word wrap
Page 3

Doc 1 Pg 1 Ln 1" Pos 1.3"

Setup: Environment

    1 - Backup Options

    2 - Beep Options

    3 - Cursor Speed   50 cps

    4 - Document Management/Summary

    5 - Fast Save (unformatted)   Yes

    6 - Hyphenation   External Dictionary/Rules

    7 - Prompt for Hyphenation   When Required

    8 - Units of Measure

    9 - Alternate Keyboard   No
        ⟨F1 - Help, Esc - Cancel, F3 - Repeat⟩

Selection: 0

*Changing the unit
of measure*
Page 7

01-15-91 07:19p   Directory C:\WP51*.*
Document size: 622 Free: 7,675,904 Used: 3,413,568   Files: 104

    .   Current   ⟨Dir⟩   ..   Parent   ⟨Dir⟩
  LEARN   .   ⟨Dir⟩ 01-15-91 02:39p 8514A   .VRS   4,860 06-29-90 12:00p
  ALTRNAT .WPK   919 06-29-90 12:00p APLASPLU.PRS   45,697 01-15-91 03:02p
  ARROW-22.WPG   187 06-29-90 12:00p ATI   .VRS   12,852 06-29-90 12:00p
  BALLOONS.WPG   3,187 06-29-90 12:00p BANNER-3.WPG   719 06-29-90 12:00p
  BICYCLE .WPG   607 06-29-90 12:00p BKGRND-1.WPG   11,391 06-29-90 12:00p
  BORDER-8.WPG   215 06-29-90 12:00p BULB   .WPG   2,101 06-29-90 12:00p
  BURST-1 .WPG   819 06-29-90 12:00p BUTTRFLY.WPG   5,349 06-29-90 12:00p
  CALC   .WPM   7,972 06-29-90 12:00p CALENDAR.WPG   371 06-29-90 12:00p
  CERTIF .WPG   679 06-29-90 12:00p CHARACTR.DOC   47,099 06-29-90 12:00p
  CHKBOX-1.WPG   653 06-29-90 12:00p CLOCK   .WPG   1,811 06-29-90 12:00p
  CNTRCT-2.WPG   2,753 06-29-90 12:00p CODES   .WPM   7,403 06-29-90 12:00p
  CONVERT .EXE 109,229 06-29-90 12:00p CURSOR .COM   1,452 06-29-90 12:00p
  DEVICE-2.WPG   657 06-29-90 12:00p DIPLOMA .WPG   2,413 06-29-90 12:00p
  EGA512 .FRS   3,584 06-29-90 12:00p EGAITAL .FRS   3,584 06-29-90 12:00p
  EGASMC .FRS   3,584 06-29-90 12:00p EGAUND .FRS   3,584 06-29-90 12:00p
  EHANDLER.PS   2,797 08-24-90 12:00p ENDFOOT .WPM   3,953 06-29-90 12:00p
  ENHANCED.WPK   3,853 06-29-90 12:00p EQUATION.WPK   2,974 06-29-90 12:00p
  FIXBIOS .COM   50 06-29-90 12:00p FLOPPY-2.WPG   475 06-29-90 12:00p

1 Retrieve; 2 Delete; 3 Move/Rename; 4 Print; 5 Short/Long Display;
6 Look; 7 Other Directory; 8 Copy; 9 Find; N Name Search: 6

Creating a directory
Page 13

Y ou're probably sitting at your computer with the C> prompt on your screen. More than likely, you have letters and reports to write, and you're anxious to get started with WordPerfect. But first, those of you who have never used WordPerfect before need to cover some basics, such as how to get around WordPerfect's Editing screen, select features and options, delete and undelete text, save and retrieve documents, back up files, and print documents. After you learn a few fundamentals, you'll easily be able to create the documents we cover in the rest of the book.

Getting Started

We assume that you've already installed WordPerfect on your computer, and that you're ready to go. (We don't give detailed instructions for installing the program because the process is so easy. Insert the Install/Learn/Utilities 1 disk in your A drive, type *a:install*, and press Enter. Then select 1 (Basic). WordPerfect will guide you through the installation process.)

To start WordPerfect, simply type *wp* at the C> prompt. WordPerfect's copyright screen makes a brief appearance, and a few seconds later, you see this Editing screen:

Editing screen ⟶

```
-




                                        Doc 1 Pg 1 Ln 1" Pos 1"
```

Not much to it, is there? In the bottom-right corner of the screen is the *status line*, which is divided into areas called *fields*: Doc tells you which document you are currently working with (you can display two documents, but you can work with only one at a time); Pg tells you which page you are on (in this case, page 1); and Ln and Pos state your position, in inches, from the top and left margin of the page.

Status line

The only other thing on your screen is the cursor (the blinking _), a visual marker that shows you where the action is—where the next character you type will be inserted or which character will be deleted if you press the Del key.

Now let's get down to business. So that you will have a document to work with as we show you how to move around, select features and options, make corrections, and save and print files, type the following note (or you may want to create your own). In case you're new to computers, you use the Shift key to enter capital (uppercase) letters and the Backspace key to erase any mistakes. As you type, note the changes in the status line.

```
In reference to your letter of January 16, 1991, I wish to assure
you that we are doing a literature search on all aspects of the
side effects of the drug Qnifen. Research currently supports the
idea that Qnifen may indeed cause stroke. However, there are many
health factors that predispose to stroke, and these must also be
taken into consideration._




                                              Doc 1 Pg 1 Ln 1.83" Pos 3.5"
```

As each line of text reaches the right edge of the screen, the next word you type automatically moves to a new line. This is called *word wrapping*, because the words "wrap" from one line to the next. Don't be concerned if the word wrapping on your screen doesn't exactly match ours. It simply means that you selected a different type of printer when you installed the program.

Word wrap

Moving Around the Screen

In WordPerfect you can move around the screen in a variety of ways. If you've installed a mouse, you can use it to quickly move the cursor anywhere in a document. Simply position the mouse pointer at the desired location, and click the left mouse button. Or, you can use the keyboard. Try pressing the **Up**, **Down**, **Left**, and **Right Arrow** keys now. You can use these keys to move the cursor up and down one line and left and right one character, respectively. Obviously, though, moving a line or character at a time is not the most efficient way to get around a document. Here are some faster ways:

To move the cursor...	Press...
Left one word	Ctrl-Left Arrow
Right one word	Ctrl-Right Arrow
To far right end of a line	End
To left side of screen	Home,Left Arrow
To right side of screen	Home,Right Arrow
Up one paragraph	Ctrl-Up Arrow
Down one paragraph	Ctrl-Down Arrow
Up one screen	Home,Up Arrow or – (numeric keypad)
Down one screen	Home,Down Arrow or + (numeric keypad)
To top of page	Ctrl-Home,Up Arrow
To bottom of page	Ctrl-Home,Down Arrow
To top of previous page	PgUp
To top of next page	PgDn
To top of page you designate at the Go To prompt	Ctrl-Home (Go To)
To top of document	Home,Home,Up Arrow
To end of document	Home,Home,Down Arrow

Let's try using various keys and key combinations to move around the note. Follow these steps:

1. Use the **Arrow** keys to position the cursor on the *R* in *Research*.

2. Press **Ctrl-Enter** to create a page break so that you can see how to move from one page to another. Word-Perfect inserts a double dashed line and moves the word *Research* to the beginning of a new line.

Inserting page breaks

```
In reference to your letter of January 16, 1991, I wish to assure
you that we are doing a literature search on all aspects of the
side effects of the drug Qnifen.
================================================================================
Research currently supports the idea that Qnifen may indeed cause
stroke. However, there are many health factors that predispose to
stroke, and these must also be taken into consideration.




                                          Doc 1 Pg 2 Ln 1" Pos 1"
```

3. With the page break in place, press **Home,Home,Up Arrow** to move to the beginning of the note.

4. Press **Ctrl-Home** (Go To), type *2* at the *Go to* prompt, and press **Enter**. The cursor moves to the beginning of the "second page."

5. To return to the top of the note, press **Home,Home,Up Arrow**.

Now that you're "mobile," let's move on to see how WordPerfect uses the function keys (the keys labeled with *F* and a number) and the Ctrl, Shift, and Alt keys.

Keys separated by hyphens

When two keys are separated by a hyphen, such as Ctrl-Enter, press and hold down the first key, and press the second key. ♦

Keys separated by commas

When two or more keys are separated by commas, such as Home,Home,Up Arrow, press and release each key in the order in which it appears in the instruction. ♦

Page breaks

Pressing Ctrl-Enter creates a "hard" page break at the cursor, as indicated by a double dashed line. If you don't manually insert hard page breaks in a multi-page document, WordPerfect automatically inserts "soft" page breaks, which are indicated by single dashed lines. You can delete a hard page break by placing the cursor after it and pressing Backspace. ♦

Giving Instructions

At this point, you may want to take a moment to locate the templates and "keycals" (color-coded decals for the Ctrl, Shift, and Alt keys) that came with your WordPerfect 5.1 software package. The templates fit around the function keys on standard keyboards and above the function keys on extended keyboards. The WordPerfect features associated with each function key are listed on the templates and are color-coded to correspond to the Ctrl (Red), Shift (Green), and Alt (Blue) keys. (Features listed in black correspond directly to the function keys.) When you're first learning WordPerfect, these templates can be time-saving memory joggers.

Using the Keyboard

As you'll see when you try the various Ctrl, Shift, and Alt key combinations, not all the keys work the same way. For example, some function keys display a menu of options when pressed, while other function keys act like toggle switches and turn a particular feature on or off. To see how function keys work, try this:

1. Press **Shift-F1** (Setup), and the Setup menu appears.

```
Setup

    1 - Mouse

    2 - Display

    3 - Environment

    4 - Initial Settings

    5 - Keyboard Layout

    6 - Location of Files

Selection: 0
```

Six options are listed on the Setup menu. You can select options from menus by pressing the number that corresponds to the option or by pressing the mnemonic (highlighted) letter in the option name, such as **M** for

Mouse. When you select an option, you may be presented with further menus. You can back out of a menu by pressing F1 (Cancel) or the Spacebar. You can also return to the Editing screen by pressing F7 (Exit).

2. From the Setup menu, select **3** (**E**nvironment). The Setup: Environment menu appears.

```
Setup: Environment

    1 - Backup Options

    2 - Beep Options

    3 - Cursor Speed                     50 cps

    4 - Document Management/Summary

    5 - Fast Save (unformatted)          Yes

    6 - Hyphenation                      External Dictionary/Rules

    7 - Prompt for Hyphenation           When Required

    8 - Units of Measure

    9 - Alternate Keyboard               No
        (F1 - Help, Esc - Cancel, F3 - Repeat)




Selection: 0
```

Since we're in the Setup: Environment menu, let's change the unit of measure for the Ln and Pos fields in the status line at the bottom of the Editing screen.

Changing the unit of measure

3. Select **8** (**U**nits of Measure). The Setup: Units of Measure menu appears.

```
Setup: Units of Measure

    1 - Display and Entry of Numbers            "
          for Margins, Tabs, etc.

    2 - Status Line Display                     "


Legend:

    " = inches
    i = inches
    c = centimeters
    p = points
    u = 1200ths of an inch
    u = WordPerfect 4.2 Units (Lines/Columns)







Selection: 0
```

Graphic 1-6: FULL--The Setup: Units of Measure menu

4. Select **2** (**S**tatus Line Display), and then select **c** (from the Legend) to change the unit of measure in the status line from inches to centimeters.

5. Press **F7** (Exit) to return to the Editing screen.

Move around the note on your screen and watch the Pos field track your cursor position in centimeters. Then return the unit of measure to inches by following steps 1 through 5 above (selecting " for inches, the default setting, in step 4). This time, make your selections by pressing the letter (mnemonic) for each option, rather than the number.

Using a Mouse

Throughout this book, we tell you how to do things using the keyboard, because everyone has a keyboard and not everyone has a mouse. However, we will take a moment here to show you how to select features and options with a mouse. (We assume that you have installed your mouse according to the instructions that came with it, and that if necessary you have used the Mouse Setup menu to tell WordPerfect what type of mouse you have.)

Mouse pointer →

In the WordPerfect Editing screen, the mouse pointer (not to be confused with the WordPerfect cursor) is usually represented by a highlighted box the size of one character, as shown in the following screen.

Using the Mouse Setup menu

To use the Mouse Setup menu: **1.** Display the menu by pressing Shift-F1 (Setup) and selecting 1 (Mouse). **2.** Display a list of mouse types by selecting 1 (Type). **3.** Highlight your mouse type, and select 1 (Selection). **4.** If you have a serial mouse, select 2 (Port), and select the port through which your mouse connects to your computer.

You have four choices: 1 (COM1), 2 (COM2), 3 (COM3), and 4 (COM4). If you don't know which to select, try each port until you find one that works. If you have a bus mouse, skip this step. **5.** Accept the defaults for the remaining five options. ♦

Combining mouse and keyboard

You can combine use of a mouse with use of the keyboard. For example, if you press Shift-F1 (Setup) to display the Setup menu, you can select an option by positioning the mouse pointer on the option and clicking the left mouse button, rather than selecting the option number or letter. ♦

```
In reference to your letter of January 16, 1991, I wish to assure
you that we are doing a literature search on all aspects of the
side effects of the drug Qnifen.
================================================================================
Research currently supports the idea that Qnifen may indeed cause
stroke. However, there are many health factors that predispose to
stroke, and these must also be taken into consideration.
```

The mouse pointer moves independently of the Word-Perfect cursor, appearing when you move the mouse and disappearing when you press a key.

To use the mouse to select WordPerfect features and options, follow these steps:

1. With the note displayed on your screen, click the right mouse button. A *menu bar*, like this one, appears at the top of your screen:

Mouse menu bar

```
File Edit Search Layout Mark Tools Font Graphics Help          (Press F3 for Help)
you that we are doing a literature search on all aspects of the
side effects of the drug Qnifen.
================================================================================
Research currently supports the idea that Qnifen may indeed cause
stroke. However, there are many health factors that predispose to
stroke, and these must also be taken into consideration.
```

If you click the right button a second time, the menu bar disappears. The menu bar lists the features and options available in WordPerfect, arranged in *menus* according to the kind of task they represent. For example, all file-related tasks, such as saving and retrieving files, are on the File menu.

Clicking	Double-clicking	Dragging
You click the mouse button to position the cursor, pull down menus, and select options. Clicking is simply a matter of pressing and releasing the left mouse button once. ♦	You double-click to select options from menus. Double-clicking is similar to clicking, except that you *quickly* click the mouse button twice. Double-clicking is especially useful in lists (such as the List Files screen on page 13), where the first click highlights the desired item on the list, and the second click acts like pressing the Enter key. ♦	Dragging across text highlights, or blocks, the text. Start by pointing to the character at one end of the text, and then hold down the left mouse button while moving the mouse. Release the button when all the desired text is highlighted. ♦

2. With the menu bar visible on your screen, move the pointer to the File-menu name, and click the left mouse button. A *pull-down* menu appears, listing the options available on the menu. To the right of some options are the keys you can press to select that option. (The black triangles adjacent to some options indicate that selecting that option displays a submenu.)

3. Move the pointer to the Setup option, and click the left mouse button. A submenu displays the options available under Setup.

4. Move the pointer to the Environment option on the submenu, and click the left mouse button. The Setup: Environment menu is displayed.

5. Change the unit of measure for the Ln and Pos fields to centimeters, just as you did using the keyboard. (Be sure to change it back to inches before moving on.)

Editing Basics

Correcting mistakes without creating a mess is one of the big advantages that word processors have over typewriters. With WordPerfect, you have several ways to make corrections.

Scrolling with a mouse

You can use the mouse to scroll up, down, left, or right through the text in your document. Simply hold down the right mouse button, and drag the mouse pointer to the edge of the screen in the direction you want to scroll. Scrolling stops when you release the mouse button. ◆

Keeping a visible menu bar

To make the menu bar visible at all times: **1.** Click the right mouse button to display the menu bar. **2.** Move the mouse pointer to File, and click the left mouse button. **3.** Using the left mouse button, click the Setup option. The Setup menu appears. **4.** Using the left mouse button, click the Display option. The Display menu appears. **5.** Using the left mouse button, click Menu Options. **6.** Using the left mouse button, click Menu Bar Remains Visible, and then click Y(es). **7.** Click the right mouse button to return to the Editing screen. The menu bar will now remain visible at the top of your screen. ◆

Deleting and Undeleting Text

You may already be familiar with the Backspace key (←), which deletes the character to the left of the cursor. To delete the character at the cursor, you can use the Del (Delete) key, which is located on the right side of your keyboard. You can delete more than one character at a time by combining the Ctrl and Home keys with certain other keys. You can then delete blocks of text, such as an entire word, line, or page. The following table summarizes the various ways you can delete text:

To delete...	Press...
The character to the left of the cursor	Backspace
The character at the cursor	Del
The word at the cursor	Ctrl-Backspace
From the cursor to the end of the line	Ctrl-End
From the cursor to the end of the page	Ctrl-PgDn
From the cursor to the beginning of the word	Home,Backspace
From the cursor to the end of the word	Home,Del

If you accidentally delete the wrong item, don't panic: WordPerfect's Undelete feature was designed to avoid such catastrophies. You start the undelete process by pressing F1 (Cancel), and you can then select 1 (Restore) or 2 (Previous Deletion). If you select 1 (Restore), your most recent deletion is restored at the cursor. If you select 2 (Previous Deletion), you can scroll through your previous three deletions and restore any one of them at the cursor by highlighting the deletion and selecting 1 (Restore).

Let's make some corrections to the note on your screen:

1. Move the cursor to the word *I* in the first sentence, press **Del**, and type *we*.
2. Press **Ctrl-Down Arrow** to move the cursor to the top of the second "page," and press **Backspace** to delete the page break.
3. Move the cursor to the *c* in *currently*, and press **Ctrl-Backspace** (Delete Word). The word *currently* is instantly deleted. (So is the space after *currently*.)
4. Press the **Down Arrow** key once, and notice how the words rewrap to adjust to your editing.

5. Next, move the cursor to the beginning of the last line of the note, and press **Ctrl-End** (Delete EOL). The last line is deleted.

6. Oops. That's not what you meant to do! To undelete the line, press **F1** (Cancel), and select **1** (**R**estore).

Restoring deletions

Now, suppose you have second thoughts about deleting the word *currently*. To undelete it, follow these steps:

1. Move the cursor back to the *s* at the start of *supports*.

2. Press **F1** (Cancel), and select **2** (**P**revious Deletion). The word *currently* reappears at the cursor.

3. Select **1** (**R**estore) to undelete *currently*.

Overtyping Errors

Another way to correct minor errors is to use WordPerfect's Typeover feature to overtype mistakes. Let's make a simple correction using Typeover:

1. Move the cursor to the *1* in *16*.

2. Press the **Ins** key to turn on WordPerfect's Typeover feature. A *Typeover* message appears in the bottom-left corner of your screen.

3. Type *28*.

4. Press the **Ins** key again to turn off Typeover. The *Typeover* message disappears.

Saving Your Documents

You probably know that the note you have typed and edited currently exists in your computer's memory and that this memory (called *RAM* for *random access memory*) is temporary. All information in RAM is wiped out when you turn off the computer. To move the note to a more permanent storage place, you have to save it. However, before we can take you through the steps for saving a document, we need to discuss a few file fundamentals.

Specifying a Directory

When you save a document, WordPerfect stores it in the WordPerfect directory (C:\WP51) unless you specify a different directory. You may want to store your documents in a directory other than WP51 to avoid confusion about which files came with WordPerfect and which you have created.

Before you save the note you have been working with, take a minute to create a directory for the documents you'll use as you read this book. If you follow the steps below, Word-Perfect automatically stores your documents in a directory called FILES. To create the FILES directory:

1. Press **F5** (List), and then press **Enter**. The List Files screen appears, displaying the files in the main Word-Perfect directory, C:\WP51.

Creating a directory

```
01-15-91  07:19p              Directory C:\WP51\*.*
Document size:      622  Free: 7,675,904 Used:  3,413,568     Files:     104

_.    Current    <Dir>                │  ..    Parent    <Dir>
 LEARN    .       <Dir>  01-15-91 02:39p │ 8514A   .VRS    4,860  06-29-90 12:00p
 ALTRNAT .WPK       919  06-29-90 12:00p │ APLASPLU.PRS   45,697  01-15-91 03:02p
 ARROW-22.WPG       187  06-29-90 12:00p │ ATI     .VRS   12,852  06-29-90 12:00p
 BALLOONS.WPG     3,187  06-29-90 12:00p │ BANNER-3.WPG      719  06-29-90 12:00p
 BICYCLE .WPG       607  06-29-90 12:00p │ BKGRND-1.WPG   11,391  06-29-90 12:00p
 BORDER-8.WPG       215  06-29-90 12:00p │ BULB    .WPG    2,101  06-29-90 12:00p
 BURST-1 .WPG       819  06-29-90 12:00p │ BUTTRFLY.WPG    5,349  06-29-90 12:00p
 CALC    .WPM     7,972  06-29-90 12:00p │ CALENDAR.WPG      371  06-29-90 12:00p
 CERTIF  .WPG       679  06-29-90 12:00p │ CHARACTR.DOC   47,099  06-29-90 12:00p
 CHKBOX-1.WPG       653  06-29-90 12:00p │ CLOCK   .WPG    1,811  06-29-90 12:00p
 CNTRCT-2.WPG     2,753  06-29-90 12:00p │ CODES   .WPM    7,403  06-29-90 12:00p
 CONVERT .EXE   109,229  06-29-90 12:00p │ CURSOR  .COM    1,452  06-29-90 12:00p
 DEVICE-2.WPG       657  06-29-90 12:00p │ DIPLOMA .WPG    2,413  06-29-90 12:00p
 EGA512  .FRS     3,584  06-29-90 12:00p │ EGAITAL .FRS    3,584  06-29-90 12:00p
 EGASMC  .FRS     3,584  06-29-90 12:00p │ EGAUND  .FRS    3,584  06-29-90 12:00p
 EHANDLER.PS      2,797  08-24-90 12:00p │ ENDFOOT .WPM    3,953  06-29-90 12:00p
 ENHANCED.WPK     3,853  06-29-90 12:00p │ EQUATION.WPK    2,974  06-29-90 12:00p
 FIXBIOS .COM        50  06-29-90 12:00p ▼ FLOPPY-2.WPG      475  06-29-90 12:00p

1 Retrieve; 2 Delete; 3 Move/Rename; 4 Print; 5 Short/Long Display;
6 Look; 7 Other Directory; 8 Copy; 9 Find; N Name Search: 6
```

2. From the List Files menu at the bottom of the screen, select **7** (**O**ther Directory).

3. At the *New directory =* prompt, type *c:\wp51\files*, and press **Enter**.

4. At the *Create c:\wp51\files?* prompt, select **Y**(es).

5. Press **F7** (Exit) to return to the Editing screen.

6. Now, press **Shift-F1** (Setup).

7. Select **6** (**L**ocation of Files) and then **7** (**D**ocuments).

8. Type *c:\wp51\files*, press **Enter**, and then press **F7** (Exit) to return to the Editing screen.

Now every time you save a document, WordPerfect will store it in the C:\WP51\FILES directory.

Saving a Document for the First Time

Naming files

When you tell WordPerfect to save a document, the program asks you to supply a filename. Using up to eight characters, you should try to come up with a name that bears some relationship to the document you're saving. And you should be consistent. For example, you might want to assign similar names to documents connected with the same project, so that they are readily identifiable as part of that project.

Enough philosophizing. Let's save the note:

1. With the note displayed on your screen, press **F7** (Exit).
2. When you see the *Save document?* prompt, select **Y**(es). (Yes is the default response, so you can also simply press Enter.)
3. At the *Document to be saved* prompt, type the filename and the extension (use *qnifen.not* for this example), and press **Enter**.
4. When you see the *Exit WP?* prompt, select **N**(o) to remain in WordPerfect with a clear screen. (No is the default response, so you can also simply press Enter.)

Your monitor now displays a clear Editing screen, and you can start a new document. But before we move on, we need to discuss a few more fundamentals.

Filename characters	Filename extensions	The List Files screen display
Here's a list of the characters you can use in filenames: A-Z 0-9 ! @ # $ % & ( ) - ' ' _ WordPerfect might accept other characters in filenames or extensions, but sticking with these characters ensures that all your filenames will be valid. ♦	To further identify the contents of a file, you can add a filename extension. The extension must be preceded by a period and can be up to three characters. For example, you might use the extensions .LET (for letters) and .MEM (for memos). Do not use .BAT, .COM, or .EXE; these extensions are reserved for program files. ♦	At the top of the List Files screen is C:\WP51\FILES*.*. C:\WP51\FILES is the pathname of the current directory. The *.* specifies that the names of all the files in that directory should be listed, no matter what characters their filenames and extensions contain. ♦

Retrieving Your Documents

With the help of a function key, you can quickly retrieve any existing WordPerfect documents you've created. To retrieve a document:

1. Be sure your screen is clear and that the cursor is in the top-left corner.
2. Press **Shift-F10** (Retrieve).
3. When the *Document to be retrieved* prompt appears, type *qnifen.not*, and press **Enter**. The QNIFEN.NOT document is now displayed in the Editing screen. (Note the pathname in the bottom-left corner of the screen: C:\WP51\FILES\QNIFEN.NOT.)

Backing Up Files

To spare you the trauma of losing work because of machine failures or power outages, or because you unintentionally cleared your screen, you should regularly *back up*, or make copies of, your files. While you are creating a document, you can back it up by using the Original Backup option and then saving the file regularly, or you can have WordPerfect automatically back up your files by using its Timed Backup option. We discuss both methods in this section. We also cover how to create copies of files on floppy disks.

Saving without clearing the screen

You can save a document without clearing the screen by pressing F10 (Save), typing a filename, and then pressing Enter. That way, you can continue working on your document without losing your place. ♦

Retrieving from List Files

If you can't remember the name of the document you want to retrieve, you can select it from the List Files screen. Here's how you retrieve QNIFEN.NOT using this method: **1.** With a clear screen, press F5 (List), and then press Enter. The List Files screen appears, displaying the FILES directory, which currently contains only the QNIFEN.NOT file. **2.** Use the Down Arrow key to move the highlight to the QNIFEN.NOT file. **3.** Select 1 (Retrieve) from the List Files menu. WordPerfect instantly displays the note. ♦

Retaining the Previous Version of a Document

By using the Original Backup option to change the extension of the previous version of a document to .BK!, you can save both the current and previous versions. WordPerfect stores the backup file in the same directory as the current version.

Let's use the QNIFEN.NOT file as an example. To use the Original Backup option:

1. Press **Shift-F1** (Setup).
2. Select **3** (**E**nvironment), and then select **1** (**B**ackup Options).
3. Select **2** (**O**riginal Document Backup).
4. Select **Y**(es), and then press **F7** (Exit) to return to the Editing screen.

Now save QNIFEN.NOT by pressing **F10** (Save). If you have already saved the file, WordPerfect asks whether you want to replace the original file with the new one. The default response is No, to help you avoid accidentally over-writing a document you might want to keep. You can accept the No response and type in a new filename, or you can select Yes to overwrite the original file. In this case, select **Y**(es). WordPerfect renames the original version as QNIFEN.BK!, and the current version becomes QNIFEN.NOT. If you save the QNIFEN.NOT file a second time, WordPerfect deletes the QNIFEN.BK! file, saves the second version as QNIFEN.BK!, and saves the third version as QNIFEN.NOT.

Timed Backups

WordPerfect's Timed Backup option automatically saves your work every 30 minutes. You see a * *Please wait* * message when WordPerfect is saving the file. If you are working with two documents, WordPerfect creates a backup file for each of them (WP{WP}.BK1 for document 1 and WP{WP}.BK2 for document 2). Backup files are stored in the main WordPerfect directory (WP51) unless you specify an-other directory. If you lose the current version of your work, you can retrieve the backup file and pick up where you left off. Wordperfect deletes these backup files when you end your current work session.

If you decide that 30 minutes is too long an interval between backups, you can change it as follows:

1. Press **Shift-F1** (Setup), and then select **3** (**E**nviron-ment).
2. Select **1** (**B**ackup Options), and then select **1** (**T**imed Document Backup).
3. Select **Y**(es) to continue timed backups, and move the cursor to 30. Change this setting to the desired time.
4. Press **F7** (Exit) to return to the Editing screen.

*Changing
backup
timing*

Copying Files to a Floppy Disk

Saving files on floppy disks is another important way to safeguard against losing valuable work. And unless you work on a network, saving a file on a floppy disk is the easiest way to transport it to another machine at home or in another office. To save a file on a floppy disk in your A drive:

1. Press **F5** (List), and then press **Enter**. The List Files screen appears.
2. Move the highlight to the QNIFEN.NOT file.
3. Insert a formatted floppy disk into the A drive.
4. Select **8** (**C**opy) from the menu at the bottom of the screen.
5. When the prompt *Copy this file to* appears, type *a:*, and press **Enter**.

WordPerfect copies the QNIFEN.NOT file to the floppy disk for safekeeping.

Timed backup directory	Searching in the List Files screen	Checking the A drive
To store your *timed* backup files in a different directory: **1.** Press Shift-F1 (Setup), and select 6 (Location of Files) and 1 (Backup Files). **2.** Type the name of the desired directory (for example, typing *c:\wp51\files* stores backup files in your document directory). **3.** Press Enter, and then press F7 (Exit) to return to the Editing screen. ♦	If the current directory in the List Files screen contains a large number of files, you can search for a particular file by choosing the Name Search option from the List Files menu and typing the filename. ♦	To check that QNIFEN.NOT was copied to the floppy disk in the A drive: **1.** Move the highlight to the directory (Current <Dir>) at the top of the List Files screen. **2.** Press Enter, type *a:*, and press Enter again. The directory is now A:\ and QNIFEN.NOT is displayed in the List Files screen. **3.** To return to the Editing screen, press F7 (Exit). ♦

Printing Your Documents

When you installed WordPerfect, the setup program asked which printer you were going to use with the program and copied to your hard drive the files necessary for WordPerfect to communicate with your printer. The printer we will use throughout this book is a Hewlett-Packard LaserJet Series II. If you are using a different printer, you might have a different choice of fonts. (We cover fonts in more detail on page 35 in Chapter 2.) Otherwise, you should have no difficulty in printing the documents you create as you read this book.

To follow along while we print the note, start with the QNIFEN.NOT file displayed on your screen. If necessary, retrieve it using **Shift-F10** (Retrieve). Then, to print the note:

1. Press **Shift-F7** (Print). This Print menu appears:

```
Print

     1 - Full Document
     2 - Page
     3 - Document on Disk
     4 - Control Printer
     5 - Multiple Pages
     6 - View Document
     7 - Initialize Printer


Options

     S - Select Printer                    HP LaserJet Series II
     B - Binding Offset                    0''
     N - Number of Copies                  1
     U - Multiple Copies Generated by      WordPerfect
     G - Graphics Quality                  Medium
     T - Text Quality                      High




Selection: 0
```

2. Select **1** (**F**ull Document).

WordPerfect sends the QNIFEN.NOT file to the printer, and printing begins.

Printing from the List Files Screen

You can also print documents from the List Files screen. This method is handy if you want to print several documents in succession. To see how to print multiple documents, create a new file by using **F10** (Save) to save the note as *qnifen2.not*, and then follow these steps:

1. Press **F5** (List), and then press **Enter**.
2. Move the highlight to QNIFEN.NOT, and type an asterisk (*). Then move the highlight to QNIFEN2.NOT (use the **Right Arrow** key), and type another asterisk.
3. Select **4** (**P**rint) from the List Files menu. At the *Print marked files?* prompt, select **Y**(es).
4. When the *Page(s): (All)* prompt appears, press **Enter**. WordPerfect sends QNIFEN.NOT and QNIFEN2.NOT to the printer.
5. Press **F7** (Exit) to return to the Editing screen.

Printing multiple files

Getting Help

WordPerfect's Help feature gives you on-the-spot information about WordPerfect's features and options. The type of information displayed depends on what you are doing in WordPerfect at the time.

The Main Help Menu

You can access WordPerfect's main Help menu from the Editing screen at any time. Here's how you use this menu:

1. From the Editing screen, press **F3** (Help). The main Help menu (shown on the next page) appears.

Printer troubleshooting

If your printer does not print after you have made a selection from the Print menu, check that the printer is turned on and that the cable connecting the printer to your computer is securely connected at both ends. If the problem persists, check that you have selected the correct printer, by pressing Shift-F7 (Print) and looking at the printer specified to the right of the Select Printer option on the Print Options menu (the bottom half of the Print screen). If necessary, select S (Select Printer), and use the options from the Print: Select Printer menu to change the printer definition. ◆

Printing one file from the List Files screen

To print a single file from the List Files screen, simply move the highlight to that file, and select 4 (Print). At the *Page(s): (All)* prompt, press Enter to print the file. ◆

```
Help              License #:  WP512111697          WP 5.1    08/20/90


      Press any letter to get an alphabetical list of features.

           The list will include the features that start with that letter,
           along with the name of the key where the feature is found.  You
           can then press that key to get a description of how the feature
           works.


      Press any function key to get information about the use of the key.

           Some keys may let you choose from a menu to get more information
           about various options.  Press HELP again to display the template.







   Selection: 0                              (Press ENTER to exit Help)
```

At the top of the main Help menu is your registration number (which you entered when you installed Word-Perfect) and the version number and date of issue of the WordPerfect program you're using. Below are instructions on how to use the Help feature. You can get information about WordPerfect features in two ways: You can press a letter key to call up a list of features with names that begin with that letter; or you can press a specific key (or combination of keys) that corresponds to the feature about which you want more information. Let's experiment:

2. Press **D** to display a list of WordPerfect features whose names begin with the letter *d*. The list has three columns: The first column contains the names, in alphabetical order, of WordPerfect features that begin with the letter *d*; the second column shows the WordPerfect key associated with each feature; and the third column lists the keystrokes necessary to use each feature.

3. Press the **Del** key to display information about Delete.

4. Press **Enter** or the **Spacebar** to exit the Help menu.

You can bypass the alphabetical list by simply pressing the Del key after you press F3 (Help). The alphabetical list is useful, however, if you can't remember which key(s) displays information about a particular feature.

Context-Sensitive Help

WordPerfect can give you *context-sensitive help*, by displaying a help screen that provides information about the particular feature or option you're currently using. For example, suppose you press Shift-F1 (Setup) to display the Setup menu and then decide you want to find out more about the options on the menu before you go any further. You simply press F3 (Help) to display a Setup menu with a description of Setup at the top of the screen. The message *(Press ENTER to exit Help)* in the bottom-right corner of the screen lets you know that Help has definitely arrived and that you're not actually in the Setup menu. To get information about an option on the Setup menu, select the option's number or letter. For example, to display information about Environment, select 3 or E. You can exit Help at any time by pressing Enter or the Spacebar.

Customer Support

If WordPerfect's Help feature can't answer your question, you can call WordPerfect's Customer Support. If you are using an IBM PC-compatible computer, you can call Monday through Friday from 7 AM to 6 PM Mountain time. If you are using a computer other than an IBM PC-compatible, you can call Monday through Friday from 8 AM to 5 PM Mountain time. When you call Customer Support, you should be within reach of your computer, and you should have your registration number in hand.

Following is a list of Customer Support departments and their corresponding toll-free numbers:

Installation	(800) 533-9605
Features	(800) 541-5096
Graphics/Macros	(800) 321-3383
Laser Printers	(800) 541-5170
Dot-Matrix Printers	(800) 541-5160
Other Printers	(800) 541-5097
Networks	(800) 321-3389

2

Efficient Memos

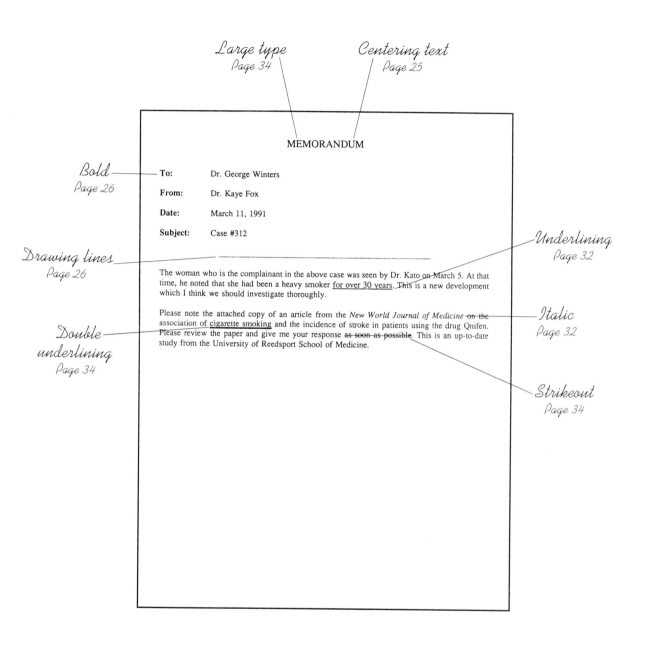

Large type
Page 34

Centering text
Page 25

MEMORANDUM

Bold
Page 26

To: Dr. George Winters

From: Dr. Kaye Fox

Date: March 11, 1991

Subject: Case #312

Drawing lines
Page 26

Underlining
Page 32

The woman who is the complainant in the above case was seen by Dr. Kato on March 5. At that time, he noted that she had been a heavy smoker <u>for over 30 years</u>. This is a new development which I think we should investigate thoroughly.

Double underlining
Page 34

Please note the attached copy of an article from the *New World Journal of Medicine* on the association of <u>cigarette smoking</u> and the incidence of stroke in patients using the drug Qnifen. Please review the paper and give me your response ~~as soon as possible~~. This is an up-to-date study from the University of Reedsport School of Medicine.

Italic
Page 32

Strikeout
Page 34

With the advent of word processors, memos are easier to create than ever before. No more scribbled or laboriously typed notes. You can now turn out—in no time at all—neat, error-free memos recording who said what to whom, calling a meeting, or announcing a new policy. In the next few pages, we show you how to create the illustrious office memo and how to set it up so that you can use it again and again, plugging in a new message each time. Using some WordPerfect features that are new to you and some that we showed you in Chapter 1, we'll first set up memo headings that really stand out. Then we'll write and edit the message, and save the memo file as a reusable template. Along the way, we'll learn about fonts and see how to use formatting to emphasize words and phrases.

Creating a Memo Template

We're going to show you how to create a memo form—called a *template*—that you can use over and over again. So before you begin typing, it's a good idea to give some consideration to the design of your memo. Most memos have a title at the top, followed by headings for the name of the person receiving the memo (To:), the name of the person sending the memo (From:), the date (Date:), and the subject (Subject:). The area below the headings is reserved for the memo message.

In this chapter, we create a plain, businesslike memo, but there is no reason why you shouldn't add a personal touch or two. After reading the other chapters in this book, you'll be able to dress up the memo template with lines or graphics.

Entering a Title

First, let's insert a title at the top of the memo document. Be sure your screen is clear. If you're at the C> prompt, type *wp* to start the WordPerfect program. If the note that you created in Chapter 1 is still displayed on your screen, press F7 (Exit), select Y(es) to save the note, and press Enter. Then select Y(es) to replace the original file with the latest version, and when the *Exit WP?* prompt appears, select N(o) to clear the screen. That's it. Now for the memo.

1. Center the cursor between the left and right margins by pressing **Shift-F6** (Center). The Pos field in the status line shows 4.25 inches (half the width of a standard 8 1/2-by-11-inch piece of paper).

2. Press the **Caps Lock** key to turn on capitalization.

3. Type *memorandum* as the memo title. As you type, Word-Perfect automatically centers and capitalizes the title.

4. To turn off capitalization, press the **Caps Lock** key.

5. To end centering and return the cursor to the left margin, press **Enter**.

6. Press **Enter** two more times to add two blank lines beneath the memo title.

Centering text

Entering Headings

When your memo title is in place, you need to enter the headings. You want to set them off from the rest of the text by emphasizing them with bold type.

In WordPerfect some formatting, such as Bold and Underline, can be *toggled* by pressing a function key once to turn it on and a second time to turn it off. Other formatting, such as Italic and Double Underline, requires a bit more effort, as you'll see in the section entitled "Filling in the Memo Template," later in this chapter.

When you turn on a format (also called an *attribute*) and type something, the on-screen appearance of that text is different from regular text, depending on the type of monitor

Starting over

If you make a mistake while creating the memo (or any other document in this book) and want to start over with a clean screen, simply press F7 (Exit) and answer N(o) to the *Save document?* and *Exit WP?* prompts. ♦

The Pos field

Turning on some Word-Perfect features changes the appearance of the Pos field in the status line at the bottom of the screen. For example, when you press Caps Lock, *Pos* becomes *POS*. Turning off the feature returns the Pos field to normal. Keep an eye on Pos, and you'll know whether certain features have been turned on or off. ♦

Formatting

We use the word *formatting* to refer to the shape, size, and general appearance of documents. Formatting can be applied to individual characters or words, as when you make them bold or italic; individual paragraphs, as when you center a heading or change the line spacing; or the entire document, as when you change the margins. ♦

you have. For example, attributes will look different on monochrome monitors than on color monitors.

To add bold headings to the memo:

Bold

1. Press **F6** (Bold), and type *To:*.
2. Press **F6** (Bold) again to turn off the bold attribute.
3. To add space between the To heading and the name you will type later, press the **Tab** key twice .
4. Press **Enter** twice to end the heading line and add a blank line below it.
5. Press **F6** (Bold), type *From:* and press **F6** (Bold) again to turn off the bold attribute.
6. Press the **Tab** key just once this time to add space after the From heading.
7. Press **Enter** twice.

Now try entering the two remaining headings, Date and Subject. Simply follow steps 5, 6, and 7. When you finish your memo template, it looks similar to this one:

```
                        MEMORANDUM


  To:

  From:

  Date:

  Subject:

  _




                                      Doc 1 Pg 1 Ln 2.83" Pos 1"
```

Separating the Messages from the Headings

Drawing lines

Before you save the memo template, you might want to draw a line to separate the headings from the message area. To create this line, you could type underscores (_) across your screen. But WordPerfect provides a more precise method of repeating characters, as you'll see if you follow these steps:

1. To center the line you are going to create, press **Shift-F6** (Center) .

2. Press **Esc** (Repeat). The *Repeat Value = 8* prompt appears. By default, WordPerfect repeats the character you specify eight times.

3. Type *50* as the repeat value, and then type an underscore (_).

WordPerfect draws a line of 50 underscores, as shown here:

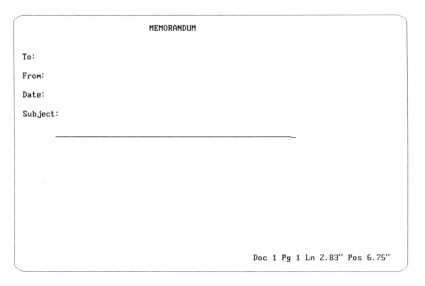

With Esc (Repeat), you can create a line that is precisely the length you want it. (You can use Esc to repeat any non-numeric character a specified number of times.)

Repeating actions

In addition to repeating characters, you can use Esc (Repeat) to repeat the actions of certain WordPerfect features, such as Delete (Del), Delete EOL (Ctrl-End), Page Up (PgUp), and Page Down (PgDn). For example, if you press Esc (Repeat), type *2*, and then press Ctrl-End, WordPerfect deletes characters from the cursor to the end of the line, twice. ♦

Changing the repeat value

To change the default repeat value: **1.** Press Shift-F1 (Setup). **2.** Select 4 (Initial Settings), and then select 6 (Repeat Value). **3.** Enter the desired repeat value, press Enter, and then press F7 (Exit) to return to the Editing screen. **4.** Press Esc (Repeat) to be sure the new repeat value has been entered properly. ♦

Canceling prompts or menus

Esc (Repeat) can be used like F1 (Cancel) to back out of prompts or menus. For example, if you press F5 (List), and then decide that you don't want to see the List Files screen, simply press Esc (Repeat), and the List Files prompt disappears. ♦

Inserting the Date

As a real time-saver, you can insert a Date code into your memo template. The Date code is an instruction that tells WordPerfect to read the current date from your computer's system clock and insert that date in the memo in the place occupied by the code. When the code is in place, Word-Perfect automatically inserts the current date in the memo every time you load or print the memo file.

To insert a Date code into the sample memo template:

1. Use the **Arrow** keys to position the cursor anywhere in the Date heading, and then press **End** to move the cursor to the end of the line.
2. Press **Shift-F5** (Date/Outline).
3. Select **2** (Date **C**ode), and the date appears.

WordPerfect will now insert the current date in every memo you write using the memo template.

Saving the Memo Template

Now that you've completed the memo template, save it for later use:

1. Press **F7** (Exit), and then select **Y**(es) to save the memo.
2. Type *memo.tem* for the filename, using the .TEM extension to distinguish the memo as a template.
3. Press **Enter**, and then select **N**(o) to remain in Word-Perfect with a clear screen.

Check that the file was properly saved by pressing **F5** (List) and then **Enter**. The List Files screen appears, displaying the MEMO.TEM file. Now press **F7** (Exit) to return to the Editing screen.

Taking a Look at WordPerfect's Codes

Whenever you use a format, such as Center or Bold, Word-Perfect inserts a code into your document. These codes determine the way your document looks both on the screen and when printed. You cannot see the codes in the normal Editing screen, but you can see them in WordPerfect's Reveal Codes screen. By activating this screen, you can check the position of your formatting codes to be sure your

document will appear on the printed page exactly the way
you want it to.

To display the Reveal Codes screen, follow these steps:

1. Retrieve the MEMO.TEM file by pressing **Shift-F10**
   (Retrieve) and typing *memo.tem*.

2. When the memo template appears on your screen,
   press **Alt-F3** (Reveal Codes), or press F11 if you have
   an extended keyboard. The screen splits in two, with
   the template displayed in both halves, as shown here:

```
                          MEMORANDUM
   _

To:

From:

Date:      March 11, 1991

Subject:

C:\WP51\FILES\MEMO.TEM                        Doc 1 Pg 1 Ln 1" Pos 1"
{    ▲   ▲   ▲   ▲  ▲   ▲   ▲   ▲   ▲   ▲   }   ▲    ▲
[Center]MEMORANDUM[HRt]
[HRt]
[HRt]
[BOLD]To:[bold][Tab][Tab][HRt]
[HRt]
[BOLD]From:[bold][Tab][HRt]
[HRt]
[BOLD]Date:[bold][Tab][Date:3 1, 4][HRt]
[HRt]
[BOLD]Subject:[bold][Tab][HRt]

Press Reveal Codes to restore screen
```

The normal Editing screen occupies the top half of the
screen, and the Reveal Codes screen occupies the bottom
half. As you can see, the two screens are separated by a tab
ruler, in which braces represent margins and triangles represent tab stops. You can move the cursor, which is a solid
block, around the Reveal Codes screen just as you would
move it around the Editing screen.

Notice the codes [Center], [BOLD][bold], [Tab], and
[Date:3 1, 4], which WordPerfect inserted when you format-
ted the memo template. Paired codes, such as those for Bold,   ←————————
have on and off components that tell WordPerfect when to   *Paired codes*
turn the attribute on and when to turn it off.

Also notice the Hard Return codes ([HRt]), which Word-
Perfect inserts every time you press Enter. Later in the
chapter, after you have typed the text of the memo, you'll
also see Soft Return codes ([SRt]), which indicate line breaks

inserted by WordPerfect. They are called *soft returns* because their position changes as you edit the document.

Don't be intimidated by all the coding. If you're like most people, when you get used to the codes, you will think nothing of flipping between the Editing screen and the Reveal Codes screen. You might even find editing and formatting documents in the Reveal Codes screen just as easy as in the Editing screen. We'll return to the Reveal Codes screen periodically throughout the book to help you become more familiar with WordPerfect's formatting codes. For now, press **Alt-F3** (Reveal Codes) to return to the normal Editing screen.

Filling In the Memo Template

Having created the memo template, you can load the file and use it at any time, by filling in the To, From, and Subject lines, typing your message, and—most important—saving the file with a name that reminds you of what this particular memo is about. As long as you remember to save each memo in its own file, the template will always be available under the name MEMO.TEM.

For now, try typing our memo so that you can practice adding attributes, such as italic and underlining, to some of the words and phrases:

Formatting capabilities

As you fill in the memo template, we will ask you to add formatting to certain words and phrases. You can follow along, adding the size and appearance attributes we specify, but whether the formatting will be present when you print the memo is a function of the capabilities of your printer and of the fonts you have available. For example, if you make some of the words in the memo italic but the font you are using does not include italic, the italic formatting will not show up when you print the memo. The same is true if you use different font sizes (small, large, very large, and so on) when the font you are using is available in only one size. ♦

File-loading shortcut

To start WordPerfect and load an existing document (such as MEMO.TEM) at the same time, simply type *wp* followed by the name of the file at the C> prompt (for example, you could type *wp memo.tem*). ♦

```
                          MEMORANDUM


To:        Dr. George Winters

From:      Dr. Kaye Fox

Date:      March 11, 1991

Subject:   Case #312


           _____


The woman who is the complainant in the above case was seen by Dr.
Kato on March 5. At that time, he noted that she had been a heavy
smoker for over 30 years. This is a new development which I think
we should investigate thoroughly.

Please note the attached copy of an article from the New World
Journal of Medicine on the association of cigarette smoking and the
incidence of stroke in patients using the drug Qnifen. Please
review the paper and give me your response as soon as possible.
This is an up-to-date study from the University of Reedsport School
of Medicine.
C:\WP51\FILES\MEMO.TEM                        Doc 1 Pg 1 Ln 4" Pos 6.3"
```

While writing this memo, you'll learn more ways to emphasize words with formatting, and we'll show you how to quickly change the text size. Our instructions are for the memo shown above, but you can, of course, follow along with your own memo.

The first thing to do is save the file with a new name so that you do not risk overwriting the template file. We used the name CASE312.MEM (for *Case #312 memo*):

1. Press **F10** (Save).
2. Type *case312.mem*, and press **Enter**.

Now, let's fill in the headings:

1. Move the cursor to the To heading line, press **End**, and type the name of the person you're writing to (*Dr. George Winters* in our example).
2. Press the **Down Arrow** key twice, and type your name in the From heading line (we typed *Dr. Kaye Fox*).
3. Press the **Down Arrow** key four times, and type the subject of the memo in the Subject heading line (here, *Case #312*).
4. Press **Ctrl-Down Arrow**, press **End** to move to the end of the line dividing the headings from the message you'll type, and then press **Enter** twice.

Now let's type the message, which includes underlined and italic text.

Underlining →

Italic →

1. Using the memo above as a guide, type the first paragraph, pausing before you type the word *for*.
2. Before typing the next word, press **F8** (Underline) to turn on underlining. Then type the phrase *for over 30 years*, press **F8** (Underline) again to turn off underlining, and type the period.
3. Finish typing the first paragraph, and press **Enter** twice to end the first paragraph and add a blank line between the first and second paragraphs.
4. Type the second paragraph, stopping just before the word *New*. To italicize the name of the journal, press **Ctrl-F8** (Font), select **2** (Appearance), and then select **4** (Italc) from the Appearance Attributes menu. Type *New World Journal of Medicine*. Then press the **Right Arrow** key once to turn off the italic attribute.

Finish typing the second paragraph, once again, using the figure on page 31 as a guide.

Formatting Existing Text

Before you add any more attributes to the memo, we should discuss WordPerfect's Block feature. Block is used to highlight "blocks" of text as small as one character or as large as an entire document. After you have highlighted a block of text, you can add attributes, change the text size, format, delete, move, or copy the whole block in one operation.

Turning off attributes

Because size and appearance attributes have on and off (paired) codes, all you have to do to turn off these attributes is press the Right Arrow key once to move beyond the off code. You can also turn off an attribute by selecting it a second time. ♦

Bold and Underline

The Bold and Underline formats are included on the Appearance Attributes menu, so you can turn them on by pressing Ctrl-F8 (Font), selecting 2 (Appearance), and then selecting 1 (Bold) or 2 (Undln). However, because they have been assigned function keys, it's much quicker to simply press F6 or F8. ♦

Deleting attributes

The easiest way to remove an attribute is to delete its code in the Reveal Codes screen, like this: **1.** Press Alt-F3 (Reveal Codes). **2.** Move the cursor in the Reveal Codes screen to the code for the attribute you want to delete (for example, [BOLD]). **3.** Press the Del key to delete the code. (If the code is one of a pair of codes, the other code is also deleted.) ♦

Let's try formatting the second paragraph of the memo using the Block feature. We'll add double underlining and strikeout attributes to blocks of text. Try this:

1. Move the cursor to the *c* in *cigarette* in the second paragraph, and press **Alt-F4** (Block), or press F12 if you have an extended keyboard. Notice the flashing *Block on* message in the bottom-left corner of your screen and the Pos field in the status line.

2. Press the **Right Arrow** key until the phrase *cigarette smoking* is completely blocked, as shown here:

```
                        MEMORANDUM


To:        Dr. George Winters

From:      Dr. Kaye Fox

Date:      March 11, 1991

Subject:   Case #312

           _____

The woman who is the complainant in the above case was seen by Dr.
Kato on March 5. At that time, he noted that she had been a heavy
smoker for over 30 years. This is a new development which I think
we should investigate thoroughly.

Please note the attached copy of an article from the New World
Journal of Medicine on the association of cigarette smoking and the
incidence of stroke in patients using the drug Qnifen. Please
review the paper and give me your response as soon as possible.
This is an up-to-date study from the University of Reedsport School
of Medicine.
Block on                                Doc 1 Pg 1 Ln 4.17" Pos 6.9"
```

If you accidentally block the wrong text, simply press Alt-F4 (Block) again to turn off Block and start over.

Another way to delete attributes

You can delete a formatting code in the normal Editing screen by using the Backspace or Del key. When you do, however, WordPerfect displays a prompt asking you to confirm that you want to delete the code. Select Y(es) to go ahead with the deletion, or select N(o) if you pressed Backspace or Del by mistake. ♦

Quick and easy blocking

To block specific portions of text, you can use the Block feature with PgUp, PgDn, End, Ctrl-Left Arrow, Ctrl-Right Arrow, and any of the other keys and key combinations listed in the table on page 4. For example, you can use Block and PgDn to block all the text from the cursor to the top of the next page, and you can use Block and Home,Home,Up Arrow to block all the text from the cursor to the beginning of the document.

You can also block text from the cursor to the first occurrence of a specific character by turning on the Block Feature and typing the character. ♦

Double underlining

3. To add double underlining to the blocked text, press **Ctrl-F8** (Font), select **2** (**A**ppearance), and then select **3** (**D**bl Und). WordPerfect double-underlines the high-lighted text and inserts paired codes into the document.

4. Move the cursor to the *a* in the first *as* in the second paragraph, press **Alt-F4** (Block), and block the phrase *as soon as possible* using the **Right Arrow** key.

Strikeout

5. Press **Ctrl-F8** (Font), select **2** (**A**ppearance), and then select **9** (**S**tkout).

What else can we do to dress up the memo? Why not add weight to the title by changing its size? Here's how:

1. Move the cursor to the *M* in *MEMORANDUM* at the top of the memo.

2. Press **Alt-F4** (Block), and then block the entire word *MEMORANDUM*.

Large type

3. Press **Ctrl-F8** (Font), select **1** (**S**ize), and then select **5** (**L**arge) to make the memo title larger.

Now save the completed memo, using **F10** (Save) so that you can stay in WordPerfect with the memo displayed on your screen.

Printing the Memo

Before we print the memo, let's discuss fonts, which can radically affect the way your printed documents look. Feel free to skip this discussion if you are familiar with fonts; you

Striking out deletions	Redlining	Avoiding exit
The Strikeout attribute can be useful when you're drafting contracts or legal reports for review by a second party and you want to show any deletions you have made. ♦	You can use WordPerfect's Redline feature on the Appearance Attributes menu in conjunction with Strikeout to denote any *additions* you have made to a document. Redlined text usually appears as broken type or on a shaded background when it is printed. To use the Redline feature, press Ctrl-F8 (Font), select 2 (Appearance), and then select 8 (Redln). ♦	If you inadvertently press F7 (Exit) instead of F10 (Save) when trying to save a document, simply answer the prompts as usual, and when the *Exit WP?* prompt appears, press F1 (Cancel). ♦

can go directly to the section entitled "Selecting a Base Font" on page 36.

Font Fundamentals

The appearance of your printed WordPerfect documents is a function of the fonts available with your printer. Every printer can print at least one font, and some printers can print several. However, you are not necessarily restricted to the fonts that came with your printer. Depending on the type of printer, you may be able to buy font cartridges (which make additional fonts available as long as the cartridge is inserted in the printer), or "soft" fonts (which you load into your computer's memory from disk so that font information can be sent to the printer along with the document), or download-able fonts (which you load into your printer's memory and are available until you turn off the printer).

You can create all of the documents in this book using the font(s) available with your printer. If we specify a font you don't have, simply substitute one you do have. In our documents, we use *Dutch* and *Swiss* because we think they give a professional look. If you don't have these two fonts, common substitutes are Times Roman and Helvetica.

Fonts come in many shapes and sizes, but all fonts belong to one of two categories: *fixed pitch* fonts (also known as *monospace* fonts) and *proportionally spaced* fonts. Courier is an example of a fixed pitch font. When you print a document in Courier, every character occupies the same amount of space. In other words, an *m* takes up the same space as an *l*, as shown here:

```
mmmmmmmmmmmm
llllllllllll
```

Dutch is an example of a proportionally spaced font, in which every character occupies an amount of space that is proportional to its width. So, an *m* takes up more space than an *l*, as shown here:

mmmmmmmmmm
llllllllll

Notice that in the Courier example, the lines contain twelve characters and are exactly the same length, whereas in the

Dutch example, the line of ten *m*'s is longer than the line of ten *l*'s, because *m* is wider than *l*.

In general, fonts are measured in terms of their height—the distance from the bottom of *descenders* (the part of letters such as *p* that descend below the line) to the top of *ascenders* (the part of characters such as *h* that ascend above the line). The unit of measure is called a *point* (abbreviated *pt*), and 1 point equals 1/72 inch. Depending on the font, you will probably use sizes between 9 points and 13 points for ordinary text and larger sizes for titles and headings. (The text in this book is 12-point, and the headings are 20-point and 14-point.)

With some printers, such as the HP LaserJet, fixed pitch fonts are measured in terms of the number of characters that print in 1 inch. In this case, the unit of measure is *characters per inch* (abbreviated *cpi*). A 10-cpi font prints 10 characters per inch, and a 12-cpi font prints 12 characters per inch. (Thus, a 12-cpi font is smaller than a 10-cpi font.) If you specified, during program installation, that you will be using a LaserJet for printing, WordPerfect automatically displays monospace font choices in cpi instead of points.

Selecting a Base Font

The *base font* of a document is the font in which the document prints. When you select a base font, you must consider the attributes you have used in the document. For example, if you've used attributes such as Bold, the base font you select must include bold. If you've used size attributes such as Large, the base font must be available in a size that is larger than the base size you select.

Because the memo you have just created includes Bold, Italic, and Large attributes, you should select a base font with all these attributes. Follow the steps below to select a base font for the memo:

1. Press **Home,Home,Up Arrow** to move the cursor to the top of your document.
2. Press **Ctrl-F8** (Font), and then select **4** (Base Font). WordPerfect displays a Base Font menu (an asterisk marks the currently selected font).

```
Base Font

* Courier 10cpi
  Courier 10cpi Bold
  Dutch Bold 08pt (HP Roman 8)  (FW, Port)
  Dutch Bold 10pt (HP Roman 8)  (FW, Port)
  Dutch Bold 12pt (HP Roman 8)  (FW, Port)
  Dutch Bold 14pt (HP Roman 8)  (FW, Port)
  Dutch Bold 16pt (HP Roman 8)  (FW, Port)
  Dutch Italic 08pt (HP Roman 8)  (FW, Port)
  Dutch Italic 10pt (HP Roman 8)  (FW, Port)
  Dutch Italic 12pt (HP Roman 8)  (FW, Port)
  Dutch Italic 14pt (HP Roman 8)  (FW, Port)
  Dutch Italic 16pt (HP Roman 8)  (FW, Port)
  Dutch Roman 08pt (HP Roman 8)  (FW, Port)
  Dutch Roman 10pt (HP Roman 8)  (FW, Port)
  Dutch Roman 12pt (HP Roman 8)  (FW, Port)
  Dutch Roman 14pt (HP Roman 8)  (FW, Port)
  Dutch Roman 16pt (HP Roman 8)  (FW, Port)
  Line Draw 10cpi (Full)
  Line Draw 12cpi (Full-Cr)
  Line Draw 12cpi (Full-LG)
  Line Draw 12cpi (Full-PE)

1 Select; N Name search: 1
```

3. With the **Up Arrow**, **Down Arrow**, **PgUp**, and **PgDn** keys, move the highlight to the desired font, and select **1** (**S**elect) or press **Enter**. (Depending on your type of printer, WordPerfect may prompt you to enter a point size.) You then return to the Editing screen.

4. When you select a base font, WordPerfect inserts into your document a Base Font code ([Font:*Font name Size*], where *Font name* is the name, and *Size* is the point size or cpi of the font you selected). Press **Alt-F3** (Reveal Codes) to see the Base Font code at the top of the memo. Press **Alt-F3** (Reveal Codes) to return to the normal Editing screen.

Additional fonts

One source of additional fonts is Bitstream. For more information about Bitstream fonts, call (800) 522-FONT, or write to:

Bitstream Inc.
215 First Street
Cambridge, MA 02142 ♦

Start at the top

Move the cursor to the top of the document before you select a base font to ensure that you select a base font for the entire document. (This small but important step is easy to overlook.) ♦

Fonts for specific elements

You can change the font for a specific text element (such as a title) by inserting a Base Font code at the beginning of the selected text and then inserting the original Base Font code at the end of the selected text. ♦

We selected Dutch Roman as our base font, because it includes bold and italic fonts. To accommodate the Large attribute in the memo, we selected 12 as the point size, because on our system, Dutch Roman is also available in 14-point and 16-point.

If you change the base font for a document, as we just did, you may have to reformat the text in your memo when you return to the Editing screen. To reformat the memo, simply press **Home,Down Arrow**.

Don't be alarmed if the memo's right margin is no longer visible on your screen. Your screen can display only 80 characters per line. When you select a font such as 12-point Dutch Roman which allows more than 80 characters to fit on each line, the lines are naturally wider than the screen, as shown here:

```
                           MEMORANDUM


    To:        Dr. George Winters

    From:      Dr. Kaye Fox

    Date:      March 11, 1991

    Subject:   Case #312


               _____


    The woman who is the complainant in the above case was seen by Dr. Kato on March
    time, he noted that she had been a heavy smoker for over 30 years. This is a new
    which I think we should investigate thoroughly.

    Please note the attached copy of an article from the New World Journal of Medici
    association of cigarette smoking and the incidence of stroke in patients using t
    Please review the paper and give me your response as soon as possible. This is a
    study from the University of Reedsport School of Medicine.


    C:\WP51\FILES\CASE312.MEM                        Doc 1 Pg 1 Ln 2.39" Pos 2"
```

To see the part of the memo that is off-screen:

Scrolling text in the screen

1. Move the cursor to the first line of the first paragraph, and press **Home,Home,Right Arrow**.
2. Press **Home,Home,Left Arrow** to return to the left margin.

You can use the Home and Arrow keys to move from one margin of the document to the other while editing the document. However, because it's difficult to work on a document that is only partially visible on your screen, you should delay making your base font selection until you're ready to print the document. While you're working in the Editing screen, we suggest sticking to a fixed pitch font, such as Courier.

If you selected a proportionally spaced font, you may also notice that the date in the memo is no longer aligned with the text in the other headings. To fix this misalignment, simply move the cursor to the first letter in the date (the *M* in *March* in our example), and press the **Tab** key. (When you restore the default font later in the chapter, you can delete the extra tab stop.)

Viewing the File

Before you print the memo, save the file and use the View Document feature on the Print menu to take one last look at your document. Although you cannot edit or format text in the View Document screen, the View Document feature is a great way to inspect your work, because you can see an entire page with all elements in place, just as they will be printed. Here's how to view a document:

1. Press **Shift-F7** (Print), and select **6** (**V**iew Document) to display the memo in the View Document screen. (If your computer does not have a graphics card, Word-Perfect may be able to display only a rough image of the document.)

2. To see how the memo will look when printed on an 8 1/2-by-11-inch piece of paper, select **1** (100%). Select 200% to display the document at twice this size.

3. To redisplay the entire document, select **3** (Full Page).

4. Press **F1** (Cancel) or the **Spacebar** to return to the Print menu.

Sending the File to the Printer

Now for the real test. After you view the memo, printing it is a one-step process:

1. Select **1** (**F**ull Document) to print the memo.

If your memo is not formatted correctly, it's probably because your printer cannot print some of the size and appearance attributes you used in the document. Otherwise, the printed memo looks similar to the one on the next page.

MEMORANDUM

To: Dr. George Winters

From: Dr. Kaye Fox

Date: March 11, 1991

Subject: Case #312

The woman who is the complainant in the above case was seen by Dr. Kato on March 5. At that time, he noted that she had been a heavy smoker <u>for over 30 years</u>. This is a new development which I think we should investigate thoroughly.

Please note the attached copy of an article from the *New World Journal of Medicine* on the association of <u>cigarette smoking</u> and the incidence of stroke in patients using the drug Qnifen. Please review the paper and give me your response ~~as soon as possible~~. This is an up-to-date study from the University of Reedsport School of Medicine.

Restoring the Default Font

Before you continue with the next section, restore the default font by removing the Base Font code from the memo. The entire document will then be visible on your screen, and you will find the remaining exercises in this chapter easier to tackle. To remove the Base Font code:

1. Press **Home,Home,Up Arrow** to move the cursor to the top of the document.
2. Display the Reveal Codes screen by pressing **Alt-F3** (Reveal Codes).
3. Move the cursor in the Reveal Codes screen to the Base Font code [Font:*Font name Size*].

4. Press **Del** to delete the code.

5. Next, realign the date by moving the cursor to either of the Tab codes ([Tab]) after the Date heading.

```
                         MEMORANDUM


To:      Dr. George Winters

From:    Dr. Kaye Fox

Date:_   March 11, 1991

Subject:  Case #312
D:\WP51\FILES\CASE312.MEM                    Doc 1 Pg 1 Ln 2.59" Pos 1.5"
{    ▲    ▲    ▲    ▲    ▲    ▲    ▲    ▲    ▲    ▲    ▲    }   ▲    ▲
[HRt]
[BOLD]From:[bold][Tab]Dr. Kaye Fox[HRt]
[HRt]
[BOLD]Date:[bold][Tab][Tab]March 11, 1991[HRt]
[HRt]
[BOLD]Subject:[bold][Tab]Case #312[HRt]
[HRt]
[Center]_____[HRt]
[HRt]
The woman who is the complainant in the above case was seen by Dr. Kato on March

Press Reveal Codes to restore screen
```

6. Press **Del**, and then press **Alt-F3** (Reveal Codes) to return to the Editing screen.

7. Press **F10** (Save), press **Enter** to save CASE312.MEM, and then select **Y**(es) to replace the original file.

More Editing Techniques

With WordPerfect, you can edit the text in your documents by deleting, moving, and copying it. We discussed the Delete feature in Chapter 1. Refresh your memory by trying this:

1. Move the cursor to the *t* in *thoroughly* in the first paragraph of the CASE312.MEM document.

2. Press **Ctrl-Backspace** (Delete Word) to delete the entire word.

Now undelete *thoroughly* so that you can see how to delete using the Block feature:

1. Press **F1** (Cancel), and select **1** (**R**estore).

2. Move the cursor to the space before *thoroughly*.

3. Press **Alt-F4** (Block), press the **End** key, and then press the **Left Arrow** key once to unblock the period.

4. Press the **Del** key. When the prompt *Delete Block?* appears, select **Y**(es), and the block of text disappears.

You can use the Block feature to delete precise amounts of text from your document. And you can restore deleted blocks of text the same way you restore any deletion—by pressing F1 (Cancel) and selecting 1 (Restore). Remember, F1 (Cancel) can restore only your previous three deletions.

Using the Move Feature

When it comes to rearranging text, WordPerfect's Move feature is really handy. It lets you move, copy, or delete an entire sentence, paragraph, or page using just a few simple keystrokes. Let's give it a try:

1. Place the cursor anywhere in the last sentence of the second paragraph of the memo.

2. Press **Ctrl-F4** (Move), and a menu appears at the bottom of your screen.

3. Select **1** (**S**entence) to highlight the entire sentence and display a second menu at the bottom of your screen:

```
To:       Dr. George Winters

From:     Dr. Kaye Fox

Date:     March 11, 1991

Subject:  Case #312
          _____

The woman who is the complainant in the above case was seen by Dr.
Kato on March 5. At that time, he noted that she had been a heavy
smoker for over 30 years. This is a new development which I think
we should investigate thoroughly.

Please note the attached copy of an article from the New World
Journal of Medicine on the association of cigarette smoking and the
incidence of stroke in patients using the drug Qnifen. Please
review the paper and give me your response as soon as possible.
This is an up-to-date study from the University of Reedsport School
of Medicine.

1 Move; 2 Copy; 3 Delete; 4 Append: 0
```

4. Select **1** (**M**ove) from the menu. WordPerfect deletes the highlighted sentence and moves it to a temporary storage place in your computer's memory. The message *Move cursor; press Enter to retrieve* appears in the bottom-left corner of your screen.

5. Place the cursor on the *P* in *Please review*, and press **Enter**. The sentence reappears in its new location. (If necessary, add a space after the repositioned sentence.)

When you select 1 (Sentence) with the Move feature, WordPerfect highlights the whole sentence, from the capital letter at the beginning to the ending punctuation (period, question mark, or exclamation point). If any spaces follow the sentence, WordPerfect also highlights as many as three of them. When you select 2 (Paragraph), WordPerfect highlights the whole paragraph, from the Hard Return code ([HRt]) preceding the paragraph to the Hard Return code at the end. When you select 3 (Page), WordPerfect highlights everything from one page break to the next.

You can use the Move feature to copy text from one part of your document to another. For practice, try copying and then deleting one of the paragraphs in the memo:

1. Place the cursor anywhere in the first paragraph of the memo.

   Copying text

2. Press **Ctrl-F4** (Move), and select **2** (**P**aragraph). Word-Perfect highlights the entire paragraph.

3. Select **2** (**C**opy). The highlighting disappears as Word-Perfect moves a copy of the text to the temporary storage location in your computer's memory. The message *Move cursor; press Enter to retrieve* appears in the bottom-left corner of the screen.

4. Move the cursor to the *T* in *The* at the beginning of the first paragraph, and press **Enter**.

WordPerfect inserts the copy of the paragraph at the cursor, as shown here:

```
Subject:  Case #312

       _____

The woman who is the complainant in the above case was seen by Dr.
Kato on March 5. At that time, he noted that she had been a heavy
smoker for over 30 years. This is a new development which I think
we should investigate thoroughly.

The woman who is the complainant in the above case was seen by Dr.
Kato on March 5. At that time, he noted that she had been a heavy
smoker for over 30 years. This is a new development which I think
we should investigate thoroughly.

Please note the attached copy of an article from the New World
Journal of Medicine on the association of cigarette smoking and the
incidence of stroke in patients using the drug Qnifen. This is an
up-to-date study from the University of Reedsport School of
Medicine. Please review the paper and give me your response as soon
as possible.


C:\WP51\FILES\CASE312.MEM              Doc 1 Pg 1 Ln 3.2" Pos 1"
```

To delete the copied paragraph using the Move feature:

1. Place the cursor anywhere in either of the duplicated paragraphs.
2. Press **Ctrl-F4** (Move), and select **2** (**P**aragraph) to highlight the entire paragraph.
3. Select **3** (**D**elete), and the highlighted paragraph is deleted instantly.

If you make a mistake while using the Delete option of the Move feature, you can correct it by pressing F1 (Cancel).

After all those changes, press **F10** (Save), press **Enter**, and then select **Y**(es) to save the CASE312.MEM file.

Using Move and Block Together

As you become more familiar with WordPerfect, you'll find that you can combine the Move and Block features to re-arrange text in a number of different ways. To get a feel for the flexibility of this feature duo, try the following, again using the example memo:

1. Place the cursor on the space before *for over 30 years.*
2. Press **Alt-F4** (Block), and block *for over 30 years* up to, but not including, the period.
3. Press **Ctrl-F4** (Move). When Block is turned on, the Move menu no longer includes options for selecting a sentence, paragraph, or page.
4. Select **1** (Block) from the menu, and then select **2** (Copy). The highlight disappears, and the message

Appending text

You can add text from the document on the screen to an existing file on disk by using the Move option called Append: **1.** Press Ctrl-F4 (Move), and select 1 (Sentence), 2 (Paragraph), or 3 (Page). **2.** Select 4 (Append), type the name of the file on disk, and press Enter. The text is then added to the end of the file on disk. ♦

Blocking with a mouse

You can block text with a mouse by holding down the left mouse button and dragging the mouse pointer across the text you want to block. ♦

Blocking spaces

When you block and move text, you need to pay attention to the spaces at the beginning and/or end of the block. Otherwise, you may end up with too many spaces in some places and not enough in others. With practice, you'll soon be able to judge which spaces to include in the block. ♦

Move cursor; press Enter to retrieve appears in the bottom-left corner of the screen.

5. Move the cursor to the period after the word *Qnifen* in the second paragraph, and press **Enter**. The blocked text is copied, formatting, spaces, and all.

Before you leave this chapter, save the sample memo one more time. Use **F7** (Exit), instead of F10 (Save), so that you can begin Chapter 3 with a clear Editing screen.

We've covered a lot of ground in just a few pages and have introduced some of WordPerfect's most often-used formatting, printing, and editing features. At this point, you might feel a bit overwhelmed. But after you use these features a few times, you'll find that WordPerfect is not nearly as memory-intensive as it may first appear and that using its features and options comes quite naturally with a bit of practice.

3

Business Letters

Fox & Associates
Medical Malpractice Consultants
1224 Evergreen Road
Lake Oswego, OR 97035

March 25, 1991

Mr. David Robertson
Sullivan, Duffy and Bridge, Attorneys at Law
145 Salmon St.
Portland, OR 97201

RE: Case #312, Rebecca Brand v. Midvalley Clinic

Dear Mr. Robertson:

Dr. George Winters and I have reviewed the medical files in the above case
and have come to an opinion. We conclude that Rebecca Brand's stroke may
have been exacerbated by her use of the drug Qnifen. However, in her case
other risk factors may have been equally or more important.

A number of case reports have associated stroke with Qnifen administration
over several years. Patient's taking Qnifen are frequently also taking many
other drugs; however, the association of stroke with these drugs in the absence
of Qnifen has not been documented.

The other risk factors that may also have played a role in Rebecca Brand's
stroke are the following:

    1. She is more than 59 years old.

    2. She has smoked cigarettes for over 30 years

    3. She has mild hypertension.

Age, smoking, and hypertension are well-known risk factors for stroke.

I hope this summary of our opinion will be of help to you. Please call upon me
for further information should you require it.

Sincerely,

Kaye E. Fox, Ph.D.

Ensuring accuracy
Page 49

Left justification
Page 55

Double spacing
Page 59

Indenting with tabs
Page 62

Single spacing
Page 60

W hether you're writing letters for business or personal use, WordPerfect can simplify the entire process by making light work of tasks such as adjusting margins and detecting and correcting spelling errors. In this chapter, we build on what you learned in Chapter 2 and show you how to prepare a professional-looking letter using some familiar features and some new ones.

The letter we use for the exercises in this chapter is shown below. Start by typing this letter or one of your own. To follow along, you must include misspellings, double words (such as *the the*), and mixed-up cases (such as *tHe*), and you should include a numbered list. Be sure to press the **Enter** key to add any necessary blank lines. If at any time you want to start over, simply press F7 (Exit), and select N(o) when the *Save document?* and *Exit WP?* prompts appear. Save the letter with a name like CASE312.LET, by pressing **F10** (Save), typing *case312.let*, and then pressing **Enter**.

```
Fox & Associates
Medical Malpractice Consultants
1224 Evergreen Road
Lake Oswego, OR 97035

March 25, 1991

Mr. David Robertson
Sullivan, Duffy and Bridge, Attorneys at Law
145 Salmon St.
Portland, OR 97201

RE: Case #312, Rebecca Brand v. Midvalley Clinic

Dear Mr. Robertson:

Dr. George Winters and I have reviewe the medical files in the
above case and have come to an opinion. We conclude that Rebecca
Brand's stroke may have been exacerbated by her use of the drug
Qnifan. However, in her case other risk factors may have been
equally or more important.

A number of case repurts have associated stroke with Qnifan
administration over several years. Patient's taking Qnifan are
frequently also taking many other drugs; however, the the
association of stroke with these drugs in the absence of Qnifan has
not been documented.

tHe other risk factors that may also have played a role in Rebecca
Brand's stroke are the following:

1. She is more than 59 years old.
2. She has smoked cigarettes for over 30 years.
3. She has mald hypertension.
Age, smoking, and hypertension are well-known risk factors for
stroke.

I hope this summary of our opinion will be of help to you. Please
call upon me for further information should you require it.

Sincerely,


Kaye E. Fox, Ph.D.
```

Fine - Tuning the Letter's Contents

Before you modify the way any document looks, you should be sure it accurately says what you want it to say. If you spend time formatting a letter so that it fits on one page and then make major content changes, such as adding a paragraph, your formatting efforts may be wasted. In this section, the changes you'll make are small, but they are significant in terms of the impression your letter will make on its readers. We show you how to use the powerful Search and Replace features and then how to put the Speller program through its paces. With these features at your fingertips, you'll be able to mop up errors and fix inconsistencies in no time.

Ensuring accuracy

Searching for and Replacing Text

With the Search feature, you can move quickly to any location within a document by giving WordPerfect a word, phrase, or code to find (called a *search string*). You use the Replace feature in conjunction with the Search feature to replace a specific word, phrase, or code located by Search with a new word, phrase, or code.

Let's use the Search feature in the CASE312.LET document to locate the word *Qnifan*:

1. Press **Home,Home,Up Arrow** to be sure the cursor is at the beginning of the letter.

Case counts

When you use Search or Replace, keep in mind that using lowercase letters in you r search string matches both lowercase and uppercase letters, whereas using uppercase letters matches only uppercase letters. For example, the search string *cat* finds *cat* and *Cat*, but the search string *Cat* finds only *Cat*. ♦

Directing your search

You can change the direction of your search while the Search prompt is displayed on your screen by pressing either Up Arrow (searches backward) or Down Arrow (searches forward). ♦

Blocking with Search

To block text from the cursor to the next occurrence of a search string: **1.** Move the cursor to the beginning of the text to be blocked. **2.** Press Alt-F4 (Block), press F2 (♦Search), and type the string. **3.** Press F2 (♦Search) again to block the text from the cursor to the end of the first occurrence of the search string. **4.** Press F1 (Cancel) to turn off Block. ♦

2. Press **F2** (◆Search), and the Search prompt appears in the bottom-left corner of the screen.

```
Dear Mr. Robertson:

Dr. George Winters and I have reviewe the medical files in the
above case and have come to an opinion. We conclude that Rebecca
Brand's stroke may have been exacerbated by her use of the drug
Qnifan. However, in her case other risk factors may have been
equally or more important.

A number of case repurts have associated stroke with Qnifan
administration over several years. Patient's taking Qnifan are
-> Srch: _
```

3. Type *Qnifan* at the prompt, and press **F2** (◆Search) again. The cursor instantly moves to the space after the first occurrence of *Qnifan*, as shown here:

```
Sullivan, Duffy and Bridge, Attorneys at Law
145 Salmon St.
Portland, OR 97201

RE: Case #312, Rebecca Brand v. Midvalley Clinic

Dear Mr. Robertson:

Dr. George Winters and I have reviewe the medical files in the
above case and have come to an opinion. We conclude that Rebecca
Brand's stroke may have been exacerbated by her use of the drug
Qnifan. However, in her case other risk factors may have been
equally or more important.

A number of case repurts have associated stroke with Qnifan
administration over several years. Patient's taking Qnifan are
frequently also taking many other drugs; however, the the
association of stroke with these drugs in the absence of Qnifan has
not been documented.

tHe other risk factors that may also have played a role in Rebecca
Brand's stroke are the following:

1. She is more than 59 years old.
C:\WP51\FILES\CASE312.LET                      Doc 1 Pg 1 Ln 4.17" Pos 1.6"
```

4. Press **F2** (◆Search) two more times, and the cursor moves to the second occurrence of *Qnifan*.

5. Now press **Shift-F2** (◀Search) twice, and the cursor moves back to the first occurrence of *Qnifan*.

If you have been following along with previous examples, you know that the word *Qnifan* should actually be *Qnifen*. You can quickly correct this error by. using the Replace feature, as follows:

1. Press **Home,Home,Up Arrow** to move the cursor to the beginning of the document.

2. Press **Alt-F2** (Replace). The prompt *w/Confirm?* appears in the bottom-left corner of the screen. If you select N(o), WordPerfect replaces every occurrence of the search string with the replacement string. If you

select Y(es), WordPerfect pauses at each occurrence of the search string and asks whether you want to replace it or not. We want to replace every occurrence of *Qnifan*, but for this example, select **Y**(es) so that you can proceed step by step.

3. When the Search prompt appears, type *Qnifan*.

4. Press **F2** (◆Search), and when the prompt *Replace with* appears, type *Qnifen*.

5. Press **F2** (◆Search) again, and the cursor moves to the first occurrence of the word *Qnifan*.

6. When the prompt *Confirm?* appears, select **Y**(es) to replace *Qnifan* with *Qnifen*. Repeat this procedure until all four instances of *Qnifan* have been replaced with *Qnifen*.

To be sure that all of the *Qnifans* have been changed to *Qnifens*:

1. Press **Home,Home,Up Arrow** to move the cursor to the beginning of the letter.

2. Press **F2** (◆Search), and type *Qnifan*.

3. Press **F2** (◆Search) again. If all instances of *Qnifan* have been replaced by *Qnifen*, WordPerfect displays a * *Not found* * message in the bottom-left corner of the screen.

Search shortcut

After you enter a search string, instead of pressing F2 (◆Search) or Shift-F2 (◀Search) to start the search, you can press the Esc key. ◆

No-confirmation caution

Be careful when replacing text without confirmation. If you accidentally misspell the replacement text, the results could be disastrous, particularly if you're working with a long document. It's wise to save your work before embarking on extensive changes of this kind, so that you can restore the original if you make a mistake. ◆

Canceling Search or Replace

You can cancel a Search or Replace by pressing F1 (Cancel). ◆

Save the letter. With all four *Qnifens* in place, the text of the letter looks like this:

```
Fox & Associates
Medical Malpractice Consultants
1224 Evergreen Road
Lake Oswego, OR 97035

March 25, 1991

Mr. David Robertson
Sullivan, Duffy and Bridge, Attorneys at Law
145 Salmon St.
Portland, OR 97201

RE: Case #312, Rebecca Brand v. Midvalley Clinic

Dear Mr. Robertson:

Dr. George Winters and I have reviewe the medical files in the
above case and have come to an opinion. We conclude that Rebecca
Brand's stroke may have been exacerbated by her use of the drug
Qnifen. However, in her case other risk factors may have been
equally or more important.

A number of case repurts have associated stroke with Qnifen
administration over several years. Patient's taking Qnifen are
frequently also taking many other drugs; however, the the
association of stroke with these drugs in the absence of Qnifen has
not been documented.

tHe other risk factors that may also have played a role in Rebecca
Brand's stroke are the following:

1. She is more than 59 years old.
2. She has smoked cigarettes for over 30 years.
3. She has mald hypertension.
Age, smoking, and hypertension are well-known risk factors for
stroke.

I hope this summary of our opinion will be of help to you. Please
call upon me for further information should you require it.

Sincerely,


Kaye E. Fox, Ph.D.
```

Directing replacements

You can change the direction of your Replace when the Search prompt appears by using the Up Arrow key (replaces backward) or the Down Arrow key (replaces forward). ♦

Code searching and replacing

To search for and replace codes, such as [BOLD] and [Tab]: **1.** Press Alt-F2 (Replace), and select Y(es) or N(o). **2.** Type the keystrokes necessary to insert the code (for example, press F6 to search for [BOLD]). **3.** Press F2 (♦Search), and at the *Replace with* prompt, enter the replacement string or code (or nothing at all). **4.** Press F2 (♦Search) to begin the search and replace. For more information, see page 88. ♦

Checking Your Spelling

Nobody spells or types perfectly all the time. Fortunately, WordPerfect's Speller feature not only detects spelling errors, but also detects double words and inappropriate capitalization. What's more, the Speller is so easy to use that you'll have no excuse for not using it on every document you create in WordPerfect.

The Speller works by comparing the words in your document with over 120,000 words in its dictionary. If it can't find a matching word in its dictionary, it displays a list of alternative spellings. You can correct the error either by selecting a replacement word from the list or by editing the word yourself. If the Speller has no alternative spellings for a word, a *Not Found* message appears in the bottom-left corner of the screen. You can then select 2 (Skip) to skip over any other occurrences of that word in your document or 4 (Edit) to edit the word.

The Speller doesn't stop for many common names, but it will pause for unusual names, such as *Sullivan* and *Rebecca*. If the name is spelled correctly, you can simply select 2 (Skip) to tell the Speller not to stop for that name again.

If you did not install the Speller files when you installed WordPerfect, you must do so before continuing with the exercises in this chapter. Then with the letter displayed on your screen, follow these steps to check your spelling:

1. Press **Home,Home,Up Arrow** to move the cursor to the beginning of the letter.

2. Press **Ctrl-F2** (Spell). The Speller menu appears across the bottom of the screen, as shown here:

```
Dr. George Winters and I have review the medical files in the
above case and have come to an opinion. We conclude that Rebecca
Brand's stroke may have been exacerbated by her use of the drug
Qnifan. However, in her case other risk factors may have been
equally or more important.

A number of case repurts have associated stroke with Qnifan
administration over several years. Patient's taking Qnifan are
Check: 1 Word; 2 Page; 3 Document; 4 New Sup. Dictionary; 5 Look Up; 6 Count: 0
```

3. Select **3** (**D**ocument) to spell-check the entire letter.

4. When the Speller stops on the names *Sullivan*, *Rebecca*, and *Midvalley*, simply select **2** (Skip) from the menu that now appears at the bottom of the screen.

5. When the Speller stops on *reviewe*, select *reviewed* from the list of alternative spellings, by selecting **B**, its corresponding letter.

```
RE: Case #312, Rebecca Brand v. Midvalley Clinic

Dear Mr. Robertson:

Dr. George Winters and I have revieue the medical files in the
above case and have come to an opinion. We conclude that Rebecca
Brand's stroke may have been exacerbated by her use of the drug
Qnifan. However, in her case other risk factors may have been
equally or more important.

                                          Doc 1 Pg 1 Ln 3.67" Pos 4"
{   ▲   ▲   ▲   ▲   ▲   ▲   ▲   ▲   ▲   ▲   ▲   ▲   }   ▲   ▲

    A. review            B. reviewed           C. reviewer
    D. reviews           E. rave               F. reavou
    G. reeve             H. rev                I. revue
    J. reweave           K. rewove             L. rive
    M. rove



Not Found: 1 Skip Once; 2 Skip; 3 Add; 4 Edit; 5 Look Up; 6 Ignore Numbers: 0
```

6. When the Speller stops on *Qnifen*, select **2** (Skip), and when it stops on *repurts*, select *reports* from the list of alternative spellings.

7. When the Speller stops on the double words *the the*, select **3** (Delete 2nd) from the menu at the bottom of the screen (see below), to delete the second *the*.

```




Double Word: 1 2 Skip; 3 Delete 2nd; 4 Edit; 5 Disable Double Word Checking_
```

8. When the Speller stops on *tHe*, select **3** (Replace) to correct the capitalization error, and when the Speller stops on *mald*, select *mild* from the list of alternative spellings. Finally, when the Speller stops on the proper name *Kaye,* select **2** (Skip).

9. A message displaying the number of words in the letter appears at the bottom of the screen along with the prompt *Press any key to continue*. Press any key to return to the normal Editing screen, and then press **F10** (Save) to save the corrected letter.

Fine-Tuning the Letter's Appearance

The letter you've typed is fairly presentable, but you can do a few things to fine-tune its appearance. In this section, we show you how to format whole paragraphs by changing justification, margins, line spacing, and indentation.

Justifying Text

The way you justify, or align, your text affects the way it looks and can determine its impact. The word *justification* means to arrange lines of text in such a way that all the lines come out even at one or both of the margins. WordPerfect offers four justification types: Full, Left, Right, and Center.

This is an example of full justification. The lines are even at both the right and left margins. Justify letters this way when you want them to appear very formal and professional.

Full justification

This is an example of left justification. These lines are even at the left margin and uneven (ragged) at the right margin. Justify letters this way when you want them to appear more informal and friendly.

Left justification

This an example of right justification. These lines are even at the right margin and uneven at the left margin. This type of justification is rarely used in letters.

Right justification

This is an example of center justification. These lines are centered between the left and right margins. Unlike the Center feature, which can center only a single line at a time, Center Justification is great for centering multiple lines of text (perhaps to draw attention to one paragraph in a letter).

Center justification

When you start WordPerfect, Full Justification is the default, meaning that if you print the letter now, the lines will be even with both margins, as they are in the previous graphic. If you want a different type of justification, you can change the setting before or after you type the document. Follow these steps to left-justify existing text:

1. To change the justification for an entire document, the cursor must be at the very beginning of the document, so press **Home,Home,Up Arrow**.
2. Press **Shift-F8** (Format) to display the Format menu.

```
Format

    1 - Line
            Hyphenation               Line Spacing
            Justification             Margins Left/Right
            Line Height               Tab Set
            Line Numbering            Widow/Orphan Protection

    2 - Page
            Center Page (top to bottom)    Page Numbering
            Force Odd/Even Page            Paper Size/Type
            Headers and Footers           Suppress
            Margins Top/Bottom

    3 - Document
            Display Pitch             Redline Method
            Initial Codes/Font        Summary

    4 - Other
            Advance                   Overstrike
            Conditional End of Page   Printer Functions
            Decimal Characters        Underline Spaces/Tabs
            Language                  Border Options

Selection: 0
```

3.　Select **1** (**L**ine) from the Format menu to display this Line Format menu:

```
Format: Line

    1 - Hyphenation                    No

    2 - Hyphenation Zone - Left        10%
                          Right        4%

    3 - Justification                  Full

    4 - Line Height                    Auto

    5 - Line Numbering                 No

    6 - Line Spacing                   1

    7 - Margins - Left                 1"
                  Right                1"

    8 - Tab Set                        Rel; -1", every 0.5"

    9 - Widow/Orphan Protection        No


Selection: 0
```

4.　Select **3** (**J**ustification), and then select **1** (**L**eft) from the menu bar that appears at the bottom of the screen.

5.　Press **F7** (Exit) to return to the Editing screen.

6.　Press **Home,Down Arrow** to reformat the letter, and then save it by pressing **F10** (Save).

Let's see how the letter looks with its new format by switching to the View Document screen:

1.　Press **Shift-F7** (Print).

2.　Select **6** (**V**iew Document) from the Print menu, and the letter appears in the View Document screen. If Left

Justification has been properly turned on, the lines of text should all be even at the left margin and uneven (ragged) at the right margin.

3. Press **F7** (Exit) to return to the Editing screen.

Now let's look at the letter from another viewpoint. Follow these steps to display the letter in the Reveal Codes screen:

1. Press **Alt-F3** (Reveal Codes). Notice the Justification code [Just:Left] at the top of the Reveal Codes screen:

```
March 25, 1991

Mr. David Robertson
Sullivan, Duffy and Bridge, Attorneys at Law
145 Salmon St.
Portland, OR 97201
C:\WP51\FILES\G3-7.LET                        Doc 1 Pg 1 Ln 1" Pos 1"
{    ▲  ▲  ▲  ▲  ▲    ▲   ▲   ▲   ▲   ▲   ▲   }   ▲   ▲
[Just:Left]Fox & Associates[HRt]
Medical Malpractice Consultants[HRt]
1224 Evergreen Road[HRt]
Lake Oswego, OR 97035[HRt]
[HRt]
March 25, 1991[HRt]
[HRt]
Mr. David Robertson[HRt]
Sullivan, Duffy and Bridge, Attorneys at Law[HRt]
145 Salmon St.[HRt]

Press Reveal Codes to restore screen
```

(To return the letter to Full Justification, you could simply delete the [Just:Left] code. However, you should leave it in place for now.)

2. Press **Alt-F3** (Reveal Codes) again to return to the Editing screen.

Page 58 shows how the letter would look if you printed it.

Justifying before typing

When you start a new document on a clean Editing screen, you can change the justification before you begin typing by following steps 2 through 5 above. ♦

Justification limitations

When Right or Center Justification has been turned on, you cannot use either the Center or the Flush Right (see page 74) feature. ♦

Blocking and justifying

A quick way to center or right-justify a block of text, is to simply block the desired text using Alt-F4 (Block), press Shift-F6 (Center) or Alt-F6 (Flush Right), and then select Y(es). Another Justification code (see page 58) is inserted at the end of the block to return justification to its previous setting. ♦

```
Fox & Associates
Medical Malpractice Consultants
1224 Evergreen Road
Lake Oswego, OR 97035

March 25, 1991

Mr. David Robertson
Sullivan, Duffy and Bridge, Attorneys at Law
145 Salmon St.
Portland, OR 97201

RE: Case #312, Rebecca Brand v. Midvalley Clinic

Dear Mr. Robertson:

Dr. George Winters and I have reviewed the medical files in the
above case and have come to an opinion. We conclude that Rebecca
Brand's stroke may have been exacerbated by her use of the drug
Qnifen. However, in her case other risk factors may have been
equally or more important.

A number of case reports have associated stroke with Qnifen
administration over several years. Patient's taking Qnifen are
frequently also taking many other drugs; however, the association
of stroke with these drugs in the absence of Qnifen has not been
documented.

The other risk factors that may also have played a role in
Rebecca Brand's stroke are the following:

1. She is more than 59 years old.
2. She has smoked cigarettes for over 30 years.
3. She has mild hypertension.
Age, smoking, and hypertension are well-known risk factors for
stroke.

I hope this summary of our opinion will be of help to you. Please
call upon me for further information should you require it.

Sincerely,


Kaye E. Fox, Ph.D.
```

Setting Margins

One way to balance the proportions of a letter is to change its margins. You can shorten a long letter by decreasing the margins, or lengthen a short letter by increasing the margins.

Let's add a little length to our letter. WordPerfect's default left and right margin settings are 1 inch. To change both margins for the entire letter to 1.5 inches, follow these steps:

1. Press **Home,Home,Up Arrow** to be sure the cursor is at the beginning of the letter.
2. Press **Shift-F8** (Format) to display the Format menu.
3. Select **1** (**Line**), and then select **7** (**Margins**) from the Line Format menu.
4. Type *1.5* for the left margin, and press **Enter**. (If you type *1 1/2*, WordPerfect converts it to 1.5.) Then type *1.5* for the right margin, and press **Enter**.
5. Press **F7** (Exit) to return to the Editing screen.

Notice that the text of the letter has shifted away from the left side of the screen. When you print the letter, the left and right margins will both measure 1.5 inches. Press **F10** (Save) to save the letter before continuing.

The new margin setting is controlled by the Left and Right Margin code [L/R Mar:1.5",1.5"] in your document. To see the code, press **Alt-F3** (Reveal Codes). To return to the default margin setting, you can delete the code in the Reveal Codes screen. Leave the code in place for now, though, and press **Alt-F3** (Reveal Codes) to return to the Editing screen.

Adjusting Line Spacing

Usually, regular paragraphs in a letter are single-spaced, but sometimes you will want to change the spacing for specific elements in the letter, or you might want to specify double-spacing for drafts. WordPerfect's default line-spacing setting is 1—single-spacing. Changing this setting to 2 produces double-spacing, and changing it to 3 produces triple-spacing. You can enter numbers like 1.5 or 2.4 for more precise control.

Follow these steps to double-space the numbered list in the letter:

Double spacing

1. Place the cursor on the number 1 in the numbered list (the third paragraph).
2. Press **Shift-F8** (Format) to display the Format menu.
3. Select **1** (**L**ine), and then select **6** (Line **S**pacing) from the Line Format menu.

Setting margins for a new document

When you start a new document in WordPerfect, you can set the margins before you begin typing, by following steps 2 through 5 on page 58 (substituting the settings of your choice in step 4). ♦

Setting line spacing for a new document

You can set the line spacing before you begin typing a new document, by following steps 2 through 5 above (substituting the desired setting in step 4). ♦

Flexible formatting

You can change justification, margins, and line spacing anywhere in a document by inserting the appropriate codes at the points in the text where you want formatting to begin and end. ♦

4. Type *2* for double-spacing, and press **Enter**.

5. Press **F7** (Exit) to return to the Editing screen.

Notice that all of the text from the numbered list to the bottom of the letter is now double-spaced, as shown here:

```
   taking Qnifen are frequently also taking many other
   drugs; however, the association of stroke with these
   drugs in the absence of Qnifen has not been documented.


   The other risk factors that may also have played a role
   in Rebecca Brand's stroke are the following:

   1. She is more than 59 years old.

   2. She has smoked cigarettes for over 30 years.

   3. She has mild hypertension.

   Age, smoking, and hypertension are well-known risk

   factors for stroke.



   I hope this summary of our opinion will be of help to

   you. Please call upon me for further information should
C:\WP51\FILES\G3-7.LET                        Doc 1 Pg 1 Ln 6.5" Pos 1.5"
```

It's important to remember that when you add formatting to a document, you're also adding codes. The formatting remains in effect from the point in the document where its code turns it on to the point where another code turns it off. Because you want only the numbered list to be double-spaced, you must insert a code for single-spacing after the

Single spacing

numbered list, as follows:

1. Place the cursor on the *A* in *Age* (the first word following the numbered list).

2. Press **Shift-F8** (Format), select **1** (**L**ine), and then select **6** (Line **S**pacing).

3. Type *1* for single-spacing, and press **Enter**.

4. Press **F7** (Exit) to return to the Editing screen.

The lines following the numbered list are now single spaced. Press **Alt-F3** (Reveal Codes) to see the Line Spacing codes [Ln Spacing:2] and [Ln Spacing:1] that WordPerfect has inserted in the letter, and then press **Alt-F3** (Reveal Codes) again to return to the Editing screen.

Changing WordPerfect's Default Settings

As you work with WordPerfect, you might notice that you use some types of formatting for all your documents. For example, you might always left-justify and double-space your documents. Instead of having to change the formatting every time you start a new document, you can change WordPerfect's default settings so that every document you create is left-justified and double-spaced.

Let's experiment by changing the default justification setting from Full to Left:

1. Press **Shift-F1** (Setup), select **4** (**I**nitial Settings), and then select **5** (Initial Codes) from the Setup: Initial Settings menu. The Initial Codes screen appears with a Reveal Codes screen displayed in its bottom half.
2. Now, press **Shift-F8** (Format), select **1** (**L**ine), and then select **3** (**J**ustification).
3. Select **1** (**L**eft) from the menu bar at the bottom of the screen, and then press **F7** (Exit) to return to the Initial Codes screen. (Notice the [Just:Left] code in the Reveal Codes half of the screen.)

```
-




Initial Codes:   Press Exit when done                    Ln 1" Pos 1"
{        ▲     ▲     ▲     ▲     ▲     ▲     ▲     ▲     ▲     }     ▲     ▲
[Just:Left]
```

4. Press **F7** (Exit) twice to return to the Editing screen.

From now on, every document you create in WordPerfect will be left-justified. If you want to change the justification of a particular document, you can still do so by placing the cursor at the beginning of the document, pressing Shift-F8 (Format), selecting 1 (Line) and 3 (Justification), and then selecting 2 (Center), 3 (Right), or 4 (Full). Of course, you can also change the default setting back to Full Justification at any time.

So that we all have the same justification for future examples, return the default setting to Full Justification now. Follow the previous steps to display the Initial Codes screen, and then move the cursor to the [Just:Left] code in the Reveal Codes screen. Press the **Del** key, and return to the Editing screen by pressing **F7** (Exit) twice.

When you return the default setting to Full Justification, the letter remains left-justified. Why? Because you manually left-justified the letter earlier and the [Just:Left] code is still in place. (The letter would revert to Full Justification if you deleted this code.)

Indenting Paragraphs

The formatting you've added to the letter has improved its looks, but it could still use a final touch or two. For example, we can indent the numbered list to make it stand out.

In WordPerfect, you can create several kinds of indents. You can indent whole paragraphs; you can create hanging indents, where the second and subsequent lines of a paragraph are indented but the first line is not; and you can indent just the first line of a paragraph to more clearly separate it from the preceding one. (The paragraphs in this book have this kind of first-line indent.) How much you indent is a function of current tab settings. WordPerfect's default tab settings are at 1/2-inch intervals, but you can increase or decrease these intervals using the Tab Set feature. You can also use this feature to set up to 40 custom tabs.

Indenting with tabs

WordPerfect offers easy ways to accomplish tasks—such as creating tables—for which other word-processing programs require you to set tabs, so you may never need to work with Tab Set. For now, indent each line of the numbered list in the letter by simply pressing the **Tab** key at the beginning of each line. We'll show you other indenting methods and talk more about the Tab Set feature in Chapter 5.

Centering the Letter Vertically

Letters, particularly short ones, look best when they are centered on the page. By "centered," we mean that the letter is approximately the same distance from the top of the page as it is from the bottom. You could achieve this effect by adjusting your top and bottom margins, but WordPerfect's Center Page feature makes it so easy. See for yourself, by centering the example letter:

1. Press **Home,Home,Home,Up Arrow** to place the cursor at the top of the page, before any codes.
2. Press **Shift-F8** (Format), and select **2** (**P**age). The Page Format menu appears. Select **1** (Center Page top to bottom) from the menu.
3. Select **Y**(es) to turn on Center Page, and then press **F7** (Exit) to return to the Editing screen.

It's that easy. When you print the letter, it will be centered on the page.

Printing the Letter

Well, you now have an accurate, formatted letter ready for printing. Remember, if you want to print the letter with a font other than your printer's default font, you need to select a new base font before you print (see page 36). Then save the letter, and check it in the View Document screen to be sure that the justification, margins, line settings, and indents are as you want them. Finally, press **Shift-F7** (Print), and then select **1** (**F**ull Document) to print the letter.

Now be sure to save the letter, because you'll use it again in the next chapter when you create a letterhead.

4

Great-Looking Letterheads

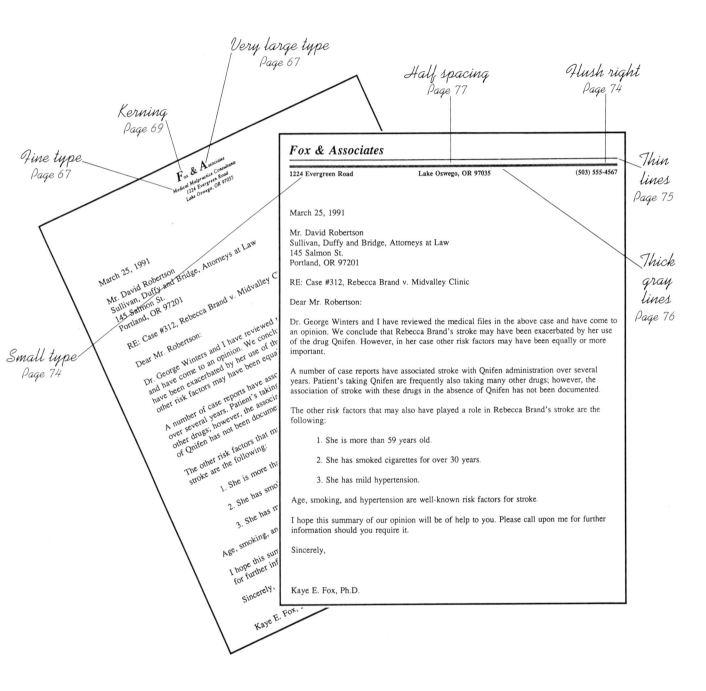

Very large type
Page 67

Half spacing
Page 77

Flush right
Page 74

Kerning
Page 69

Fine type
Page 67

Thin lines
Page 75

Thick gray lines
Page 76

Small type
Page 74

Fox & Associates

1224 Evergreen Road   Lake Oswego, OR 97035   (503) 555-4567

March 25, 1991

Mr. David Robertson
Sullivan, Duffy and Bridge, Attorneys at Law
145 Salmon St.
Portland, OR 97201

RE: Case #312, Rebecca Brand v. Midvalley Clinic

Dear Mr. Robertson:

Dr. George Winters and I have reviewed the medical files in the above case and have come to an opinion. We conclude that Rebecca Brand's stroke may have been exacerbated by her use of the drug Qnifen. However, in her case other risk factors may have been equally or more important.

A number of case reports have associated stroke with Qnifen administration over several years. Patient's taking Qnifen are frequently also taking many other drugs; however, the association of stroke with these drugs in the absence of Qnifen has not been documented.

The other risk factors that may also have played a role in Rebecca Brand's stroke are the following:

    1. She is more than 59 years old.

    2. She has smoked cigarettes for over 30 years.

    3. She has mild hypertension.

Age, smoking, and hypertension are well-known risk factors for stroke.

I hope this summary of our opinion will be of help to you. Please call upon me for further information should you require it.

Sincerely,

Kaye E. Fox, Ph.D.

In Chapter 2 you learned how to use fonts and how to change the appearance of individual characters and words, and in Chapter 3 you learned how to use justification, margins, and line spacing to change the look of whole paragraphs. In this chapter, we'll show you how to combine these formatting capabilities to create a couple of letterheads.

Most businesses use letterhead stationery. The advantage of using a computer-generated letterhead is that you don't have to switch the paper in your printer from plain bond to letterhead every time you print a letter. If you work for a company that already has preprinted letterhead, you probably have no choice about using it. However, you might want to use the instructions in this chapter to create a letterhead for your personal correspondence. As you follow along, you'll probably think of other ways you could put the letterhead techniques to work—for example, generating eye-catching advertisements or attractive flyers.

A Simple Letterhead

First, we'll discuss the centered letterhead shown on the previous page. This letterhead is simple to generate and is a good way to become familiar with the various features WordPerfect provides for creating *display type*—a fancy term for words that are intended to catch the eye.

Well, let's begin. If you're at the C> prompt, type *wp* to start the WordPerfect program. Then, with a clear screen in front of you, follow these steps:

1. To center the words you are going to type, press **Shift-F8** (Format), select **1** (**Line**), select **3** (**Justification**), select **2** (**Center**), and then press **F7** (Exit) to return to the Editing screen.
2. Type the text of the letterhead. For example, we entered the four lines shown at the top of the next page, pressing **Enter** to end each line:

```
                    Fox & Associates
           Medical Malpractice Consultants
                  1224 Evergreen Road
                  Lake Oswego, OR 97035

                           —
```

3. Press **Enter** four times after the last line, to create a buffer space between the letterhead and the text of any memo or letter you type.

Speedy Formatting

Now let's format the letterhead. Looking back at the illustration at the beginning of the chapter, you'll see that the entire letterhead is italic, with key letters in large bold type. Start with the formatting that affects the majority of the text:

1. Press **Home,Home,Up Arrow** to move the cursor to the beginning of the letterhead.
2. Press **Alt-F4** (Block), and block the entire letterhead by pressing the **Down Arrow** and **End** keys.
3. To make the entire letterhead italic, press **Ctrl-F8** (Font), select **2** (**A**ppearance), and then select **4** (**I**talc).
4. Without moving the cursor, press **Alt-F4** (Block) again, and then press **Ctrl-Home** (Go To) twice to reblock the letterhead. Then press **Ctrl-F8** (Font), and select **1** (**S**ize) and **3** (**F**ine).

Fine type

Let's tackle the individual letters we want to emphasize. In the example letterhead, we want to make the *F* in *Fox*, the ampersand (&), and the *A* in *Associates* both bold and bigger. Follow along, using the appropriate letters in your letterhead:

1. Move the cursor to the *F* in *Fox*, press **Alt-F4** (Block), and block only the *F* by pressing the **Right Arrow** key once. Press **F6** (Bold).
2. Without moving the cursor, press **Alt-F4** (Block) again, and then press **Ctrl-Home** (Go To) twice to reblock the *F*. Then press **Ctrl-F8** (Font), select **1** (**S**ize), and select **6** (**V**ry Large) to make the *F* very large.

Very large type

3. Repeat the previous two steps for the *A* in *Associates*.

4. Repeat the same steps for the ampersand (&), selecting **5** (**L**arge) in step 2 instead of 6 (Vry Large).

Before you go any further, save the letterhead by pressing **F10** (Save), typing *lh1.tem* (for Letterhead 1 Template), and pressing **Enter**. (As you'll recall from Chapter 2, we recommend that you always use the filename extension .TEM for files that you do not want to change.)

Test Printing

The next step is to choose a base font for the letterhead and print a test copy so that we can determine what adjustments we need to make, if any. We used 12-point Dutch Roman for our base font, for two reasons: to accommodate all the size and appearance attributes used in the letterhead, and for compatibility with the letter we wrote in Chapter 3. If Dutch is not available with your printer, select a font that has bold and italic and enough point sizes to accommodate Fine, Large, and Very Large sizes. And keep in mind that your letterhead might look a bit different from ours.

Follow these steps to select a base font, view the letterhead, and print it:

1. Press **Home,Home,Up Arrow** to move the cursor to the beginning of the document.
2. Press **Ctrl-F8** (Font), select **4** (Base **F**ont), highlight Dutch Roman 12pt, and press **Enter**.

Slow-moving cursor

After you format a document, the cursor may appear not to move when you press the Arrow keys. You must press the Arrow key once for each of the codes Word-Perfect has inserted. Because you can't see codes, such as [BOLD][bold] and [VRY LARGE][vry large], on the Editing screen, the cursor appears to stand still until it passes them all. ♦

Finding fonts quickly

If you don't want to scroll through all the font names on the Base Font menu, you can use Name Search to help you find a specific font. While the Base Font menu is displayed on your screen, select N (Name search), and then type the first letter of the font you're looking for. The highlight instantly moves to the first font name that begins with the letter you typed. As

you continue to type the remaining letters of the font name, the highlight moves to the first font that matches the letters you've typed. Press Enter or the Arrow keys to exit Name Search. ♦

3. To view the letterhead, press **Shift-F7** (Print), and select **6** (View Document).

4. To print the letterhead, press **F1** (Cancel) or the **Spacebar** to return to the Print menu, and then press **1** (Full Document).

Take a moment to admire your efforts, which look something like the letterhead shown here:

F_{ox} & A_{ssociates}
Medical Malpractice Consultants
1224 Evergreen Road
Lake Oswego, OR 97035

Fine-Tuning

Take a good look at the printed letterhead shown above. Notice the space between the *F* and the *o* in *Fox*. The other letters are evenly spaced, but the *F* and the *o* seem too far apart. Inconsistencies in letter spacing are the result of differences in the shapes and slants of various letters. You can manually decrease or increase the amount of space between letters by using WordPerfect's Advance feature. Adjusting the space between letters is called *kerning*. Let's use Advance to kern the *F* and the *o* in *Fox*.

Kerning

Changing the default base font

If you don't want to bother with selecting a base font every time you create a document, you can use the Initial Settings and the Initial Codes features (see page 61) to select a base font that will be used for all the Word-Perfect documents you create from that point on. (Existing documents will not be affected.)

For example, to change the base font of all future documents to Dutch Roman 12pt: **1.** Press Shift-F1 (Setup), select 4 (Initial Settings), and then select 5 (Initial Codes). **2.** When the Initial Codes screen appears, press Ctrl-F8 (Font), select 4 (Base Font), select Dutch Roman 12pt from the Base Font menu, and press Enter.

You can override the Base Font code in the Initial Codes

screen by selecting a different base font for the document currently displayed in the Editing screen. ◆

1. Move the cursor to the *o* in *Fox*.

2. Press **Shift-F8** (Format), select **4** (**O**ther), and select **1** (**A**dvance). This menu appears:

```
Format: Other

       1 - Advance

       2 - Conditional End of Page

       3 - Decimal/Align Character     .
           Thousands' Separator        ,

       4 - Language                   US

       5 - Overstrike

       6 - Printer Functions

       7 - Underline - Spaces         Yes
                       Tabs           No

       8 - Border Options




Advance: 1 Up; 2 Down; 3 Line; 4 Left; 5 Right; 6 Position: 0
```

3. Select **4** (**L**eft), type *.04*, and press **Enter**. The *o* in *Fox* is "advanced" to the left by 4/100s of an inch.

4. Press **F7** (Exit) to return to the Editing screen.

Now print the letterhead again and compare this printout with the first one to be sure that the space between the kerned letters is as you want it. (To increase the space, simply advance the *o* in *Fox* to the right rather than the left.) Then press **F7** (Exit) to save the letterhead and clear the screen.

Merging the Letterhead with a Letter

Now we're ready to merge the letterhead with a letter. In this section, we'll load the letter we wrote in Chapter 3 and then merge the LH1.TEM document at the top. Before we merge the letterhead, we need to delete the return address at the top of the letter, because it contains the same information. Follow these steps:

1. Press **Shift-F10** (Retrieve), type the name of the letter you created in Chapter 3 (we called it *case312.let*), and press **Enter** to load the letter.

2. Press **Alt-F3** (Reveal Codes) to display the Reveal Codes screen, and be sure the cursor is on the *F* in *Fox*.

3. Press **Alt-F4** (Block), and use the **Down Arrow** key to block the entire return address, including the last Hard Return code ([HRt]). Watch the Editing screen as you block the text. When you finish blocking, the cursor should be on the *M* in *March* (none of the formatting codes preceding the first line of the return address should be blocked).

```
Fox & Associates
Medical Malpractice Consultants
1224 Evergreen Road
Lake Oswego, OR 97035

March 25, 1991

Mr. David Robertson
Sullivan, Duffy and Bridge, Attorneys at Law
145 Salmon St.
Portland, OR 97201
Block on                                Doc 1 Pg 1 Ln 1.83" Pos 1.5"
     {    ▲    ▲    ▲    ▲    ▲    ▲    ▲    }    ▲    ▲    ▲
1224 Evergreen Road[HRt]
Lake Oswego, OR 97035[HRt]
[HRt]
March 25, 1991[HRt]
[HRt]
Mr. David Robertson[HRt]
Sullivan, Duffy and Bridge, Attorneys at Law[HRt]
145 Salmon St.[HRt]
Portland, OR 97201[HRt]
[HRt]

Press Reveal Codes to restore screen
```

4. Press the **Del** key, and then select **Y**(es) to delete the return address.
5. Press **Alt-F3** (Reveal Codes) to return to the Editing screen.

Now save the letter by pressing **F10** (Save). With the return address deleted, you're ready to merge the letterhead with the letter:

1. Press **Home,Home,Home,Up Arrow** to move the cursor to the beginning of the document. It's important to press the Home key three times so that the cursor is located *before* any codes in the letter. Otherwise, some of the formatting codes in the letterhead (such as center justification) will affect the letter too.
2. Press **Shift-F10** (Retrieve), type *lh1.tem*, and press **Enter** to merge the letterhead at the top of the letter.

After the merge, notice the filename in the bottom-left corner of the screen.

```
                        Fox & Associates
                  Medical Malpractice Consultants
                       1224 Evergreen Road
                      Lake Oswego, OR 97035


         March 25, 1991

         Mr. David Robertson
         Sullivan, Duffy and Bridge, Attorneys at Law
         145 Salmon St.
         Portland, OR 97201

         RE: Case #312, Rebecca Brand v. Midvalley Clinic

         Dear Mr. Robertson:

         Dr. George Winters and I have reviewed the medical files in the above case
         and have come to an opinion. We conclude that Rebecca Brand's stroke may
         have been exacerbated by her use of the drug Qnifen. However, in her case
         other risk factors may have been equally or more important.

         A number of case reports have associated stroke with Qnifen administration
C:\WP51\FILES\CASE312.LET                              Doc 1 Pg 1 Ln 1" Pos 1"
```

The merged document retains the filename CASE312.LET because the LH1.TEM document was retrieved into the CASE312.LET document. (If the letter had been retrieved into the letterhead, the filename would be LH1.TEM.)

Press **F10** (Save), and save the merged letter with a different filename—perhaps, *case312.lh1*—so that you can use the unmerged letter later in the chapter. Then print the merged letter, this time from the List Files screen:

1. Press **F5** (List), and then press **Enter**.
2. In the List Files screen, use the **Arrow** keys to highlight the CASE312.LH1 file.

Printing selected pages

If the file you are printing from the List Files screen has multiple pages, you can select any or all of the pages to be printed. Page numbers can be entered at the *Page(s): (All)* prompt as follows: if you enter 3,5 or 3 5, pages 3 and 5 are printed; if you enter 3-5, pages 3, 4, and 5 are printed; and if you enter 3,5,7-10, pages 3, 5, and 7 through 10 are printed. ♦

Viewing from List Files

To see the text of a file before you print it from the List Files screen, use the Look option on the List Files menu. To use Look: **1.** Press F5 (List), and then press Enter. **2.** Move the highlight to the desired file in the list, and select 6 (Look) from the List Files menu. The file is displayed in the Look screen. You can move around the file in the Look screen just as you would in the Editing screen, but you cannot edit the file. To display the next or previous file in the Look screen, select 1 (Next Doc) or 2 (Prev Doc). **3.** Press F7 (Exit) to return to the List Files screen. ♦

3. Select **4** (**P**rint) from the List Files menu at the bottom of the screen, and when the *Page(s): (All)* prompt appears in the bottom-left corner, press **Enter** to print the file, which should look like the letter at the beginning of the chapter.

Press **F7** (Exit) to save the merged letter and clear the screen in preparation for the next letterhead.

A More Sophisticated Letterhead

The letterhead you just created does the job, but it's very simple. Let's now explore some of the WordPerfect features that can help you create a more sophisticated letterhead. As you follow along, refer to the other letterhead pictured at the beginning of the chapter, so you can see the effect you are aiming for. Again, you can use the example name and address or substitute your own. We're going to work on this letterhead one section at a time, entering and formatting the name and address first and then dressing them up with lines:

1. We want the name to be bold, so press **F6** (Bold), type *Fox & Associates*, and then press **Home,Left Arrow** to return the cursor to the beginning of the line.
2. To make the name both bold and italic, let's add the italic attribute. Press **Alt-F4** (Block), and press **End** to block the entire line. Then press **Ctrl-F8** (Font), select **2** (Appearance) and **4** (**I**talc).
3. To make the type bigger, press **Alt-F4** (Block), and press **Ctrl-Home** (Go To) twice to reselect the block. Then press **Ctrl-F8** (Font), select **1** (Size) and **6** (**V**ry Large).
4. Press **Home,Right Arrow** to move the cursor to the end of the name, and press **Enter** to start a new line.

Here's what this line would look like if you printed it now:

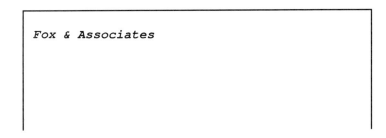

The address in the example letterhead is fairly long, and although we want to keep the bold type, we need to make the address small so that it will fit on one line. Follow these steps to create an address line like the shown on page 65.

1. Press **F6** (Bold) to turn on the bold attribute and type *1224 Evergreen Road.*
2. Press **Shift-F6** (Center). The cursor moves to the center of the screen.
3. Type *Lake Oswego, OR 97035.*

Flush right

4. With the cursor at the end of the address, press **Alt-F6** (Flush Right). The cursor moves to the right edge of the screen.
5. Type *(503) 555-4567.* Notice how the characters move backward as you type. Using WordPerfect's Flush Right feature ensures that the telephone number is aligned with the right margin.

Small type

6. To make the address line small, start by blocking the whole line. Press **Alt-F4** (Block), and then press **Home,Left Arrow**. Press **Ctrl-F8** (Font), and select **1** (Size) and **4** (Small).

That's it for the text of the letterhead. The address line might look a little crowded on the screen, but it will be fine when the letterhead is printed, as you can see here:

```
┌─────────────────────────────────────────────────────────┐
│                                                          │
│  Fox & Associates                                        │
│  1224 Evergreen Road         Lake Oswego, OR 97035          (503) 555-4567  │
│                                                          │
│                                                          │
│                                                          │
│                                                          │
│                                                          │
│                                                          │
└─────────────────────────────────────────────────────────┘
```

Adding Lines

You've created a functional but plain letterhead. In this section, we show you how to use WordPerfect's Graphics feature to dress up the letterhead by drawing two kinds of lines between the name and the address: a thin, solid black line and a somewhat thicker, gray line. When you are familiar

with basic line-drawing techniques, you can experiment on
your own, adding different lines and boxes to create the
effect you want. For now, follow these steps:

1. To create a space between the name and the address,
   press **Home,Home,Up Arrow** to move to the first line
   of the letterhead, press **End** to move to the end of the
   line, and then press **Enter**.

2. To draw the first line, press **Alt-F9** (Graphics), select
   5 (**L**ine), and then select **1** (**H**orizontal). This Graphics:
   Horizontal Line menu appears:

```
Graphics: Horizontal Line

    1 - Horizontal Position      Full

    2 - Vertical Position        Baseline

    3 - Length of Line

    4 - Width of Line            0.013"

    5 - Gray Shading (% of black) 100%










Selection: 0
```

3. Select **4** (**W**idth of Line). The default line width is 0.013
   inch. Type *.02*, and then press **Enter** to make the line
   0.02 inch wide.   *Thin lines*

4. The other settings in the Graphics: Horizontal Line
   menu are as you want them, so press **F7** (Exit) to return
   to the Editing screen.

You can't see the line you just created in the Editing
screen, but you can see it in the View Document screen, and
of course, you'll also see it when you print the letterhead.
Before you print, though, draw the next line:

1. To create a blank space and start a new line, press
   Enter twice.

*Thick gray
lines*

2. To draw the second line, press **Alt-F9** (Graphics), and select **5** (**L**ine) and **1** (**H**orizontal). Then select **4** (**W**idth of Line), type *.05*, and press **Enter** to make the line 0.05 inch wide.

3. To make the line gray instead of black, select **5** (**G**ray Shading), type *50*, and press **Enter**. (A setting of 50% means that the line is 50 percent black dots and 50 percent white dots, which creates an even gray shade.)

4. Press **F7** (Exit) to return to the Editing screen, and press **Enter** to end the line.

Save this letterhead with the name lh2.tem.

Test Printing

As with the first letterhead you created, the next step is to choose a base font and print a test copy of the file to be sure that all your formatting is in place and that the lines are positioned correctly. Follow these steps:

1. Press **Home,Home,Up Arrow** to move the cursor to the beginning of the document.

2. Press **Ctrl-F8** (Font), select **4** (Base **F**ont), use the **Arrow** keys to move the highlight to Dutch Roman 12pt, and then press **Enter**.

3. To view the letterhead, press **Shift-F7** (Print), and select **6** (**V**iew Document).

4. To print the letterhead, press **F1** (Cancel) or the **Spacebar** to return to the Print menu, and then press **1** (**F**ull Document).

The printed letterhead looks something like this:

Fox & Associates

1224 Evergreen Road   Lake Oswego, OR 97035   (503) 555-4567

Fine-Tuning

Looking over the printed letterhead above, you'll notice that it seems somewhat spread out. You can make the letterhead hang together better as a unit by decreasing the space between the lines from single-spacing to half-spacing. Let's make this adjustment by entering the necessary code, keeping our eyes on the Reveal Codes screen as we do it. Here are the steps:

1. Press **Alt-F3** (Reveal Codes), and position the cursor after the Hard Return code at the end of the name line.
2. Press **Shift-F8** (Format), and select **1** (Line) and **6** (Line Spacing). Type .5, and press **Enter**.
3. Press **F7** (Exit) to return to the Reveal Codes screen. WordPerfect has inserted the Line Spacing code [Ln Spacing:0.5] in the letterhead.

Half spacing

```
Fox & Associates
_


1224 Evergreen Road    Lake Oswego, OR 97035         (503) 555-4567



C:\WP51\FILES\LH2.TEM                      Doc 1 Pg 1 Ln 1.28" Pos 1"
{         ▲    ▲    ▲  ▲    ▲  ▲      ▲    }    ▲    ▲
[Ln Spacing:0.5][HLine:Full,Baseline,6.5",0.02",100%][HRt]
[HRt]
[HLine:Full,Baseline,6.5",0.05",50%][HRt]
[HRt]
[BOLD][SMALL]1224 Evergreen Road[Center]Lake Oswego, OR 97035[Flsh Rgt](503) 555
[-]4567[small][bold]



Press Reveal Codes to restore screen
```

4. Press **Alt-F3** (Reveal Codes) to return to the Editing screen.

Before you can merge the letterhead with a letter, you must first insert WordPerfect's default Line Spacing code at the end of the letterhead. Otherwise, the half-spacing code will affect the line spacing of the documents with which you merge the letterhead. This important step is sometimes easy to overlook. Let's enter this code through the Format menu:

1. To be sure the cursor is at the very end of the letterhead, press **Home,Home,Down Arrow**.
2. To insert a single-spacing code, press **Shift-F8** (Format), select **1** (**Line**) and **6** (Line Spacing), type *1*, and press **Enter**.
3. Press **F7** (Exit) to return to the Editing screen.
4. With the cursor still at the end of the letterhead, press **Enter** four times to insert blank spaces below the letterhead.

When you print the letterhead again, it looks like this:

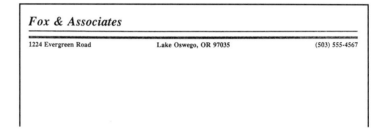

Before you move on to the next section, press **F7** (Exit) to save the letterhead and clear the screen.

Using Split Windows to Merge Documents

Now we can merge the letterhead with the example letter. This time, we'll use a different method. First, we'll split the Editing screen into two windows and load the letterhead in one window and the letter in the other. Then we'll simply move a copy of the letterhead to the top of the letter.

When you split the screen, each window has its own status line. The document in one window is designated as Document 1 (*Doc 1*), and the document in the other window is designated as Document 2 (*Doc 2*). The windows are separated by a reverse video bar, resembling the one between the Editing screen and the Reveal Codes screen. Triangles representing tab stops in the reverse video bar always point to the window containing the cursor. You move between the two windows by pressing Shift-F3 (Switch).

Follow the steps below to split the screen:

1. Press **Ctrl-F3** (Screen), and select **1** (**W**indow).

2. When the *Number of lines in this window* prompt appears, type *11*. Designating 11 lines for the first window splits the screen approximately in half.

3. Press **Enter**, and the Editing screen instantly splits into two windows.

4. With the cursor in the Document 1 window, press **Shift-F10** (Retrieve), and type *case312.let* to retrieve the letter into this window.

5. Press **Shift-F3** (Switch) to move the cursor to the Document 2 window, press **Shift-F10** (Retrieve), and type *lh2.tem* to retrieve the letterhead into the second window.

Both the CASE312.LET and LH2.TEM documents are now displayed in their respective windows, like this:

```
March 25, 1991

Mr. David Robertson
Sullivan, Duffy and Bridge, Attorneys at Law
145 Salmon St.
Portland, OR 97201

RE: Case #312, Rebecca Brand v. Midvalley Clinic

Dear Mr. Robertson:

C:\WP51\FILES\CASE312.LET                          Doc 1 Pg 1 Ln 1" Pos 1.5"
{   ▼   ▼   ▼   ▼   ▼    ▼   ▼   ▼    ▼   ▼   ▼   }   ▼   ▼
Fox & Associates



    1224 Evergreen Road    Lake Oswego, OR 97035        (503) 555-4567




C:\WP51\FILES\LH2.TEM                              Doc 2 Pg 1 Ln 1" Pos 1"
```

Now let's merge the two documents:

1. With the cursor still in the Document 2 window, press **Home,Home,Home,Up Arrow** to position the cursor before the codes at the beginning of the letterhead.

2. Block the entire letterhead, including the four Hard Return codes ([HRt]) at the end.

Copying between windows

3. To check that all the [HRt]s are blocked, press **Alt-F3** (Reveal Codes). In the Reveal Codes screen, the cursor should be located just below the last [HRt]. (When you press Alt-F3, the Document 2 window fills the top half of the screen and the Reveal Codes screen fills the bottom half. The Document 1 window is no longer visible.) Press **Alt-F3** (Reveal Codes) to return to the Editing screen.

4. To copy the blocked text, press **Ctrl-F4** (Move), select **1** (**B**lock), and then select **2** (**C**opy). The *Move cursor; press Enter to retrieve* message appears in the bottom-left corner of the screen.

5. Press **Shift-F3** (Switch) to move the cursor to the Document 1 window.

6. Press **Home,Home,Home,Up Arrow** to position the cursor before the codes at the beginning of the letter.

7. Press **Enter** to place the copy of the letterhead at the top of the letter.

Save the merged document with an appropriate name, such as *case312.lh2*, and then close the Document 2 window by following these steps:

Closing the second window

1. Press **Shift-F3** (Switch) to move the cursor to the Document 2 window.

2. Press **F7** (Exit), select **N**(o) when the *Save document?* prompt appears, and then select **Y**(es) to exit LH2.TEM. The cursor moves to the Document 1 window.

3. Press **Ctrl-F3** (Screen), select **1** (**W**indow), and when the *Number of lines in this window* prompt appears, type *0*, and press **Enter** to close the Document 2 window.

Final Touches

Because you made base font selections for both the letter and the letterhead and then saved them in previous exercises, you don't have to select a base font now. But before you print the merged letter, check it quickly in the View Document screen:

1. With the cursor at the top of the document, press **Shift-F7** (Print), and then select **6** (**V**iew Document).

Notice anything wrong? In Chapter 3, you increased the margins of the letter from 1 inch to 1.5 inches, and now the letterhead is half an inch wider than the letter on either side. You can correct this problem in the Reveal Codes screen.

2. Press **F7** (Exit) to return to the Editing screen.

3. Press **Alt-F3** (Reveal Codes), move the cursor to the Left and Right Margin code ([L/R Mar:1.5",1.5"]), and press **Del** to delete the code. The text of the letter instantly shifts to the left edge of the screen. Press **Alt-F3** (Reveal Codes) to return to the Editing screen.

Now save the merged document once again by pressing **F10** (Save), and then print it. The result should be identical to the letter at the beginning of the chapter.

Moving the Letterheads to Their Own Directory

As you know, you can use the Other Directory option on the List Files menu to organize your WordPerfect files by creating directories for specific types of documents. For example, you can create a directory called *LH* for your letterheads. Then you can move the two letterhead files from the current directory (FILES) to the LH directory using the Move/Rename option. Take a few minutes to do that now.

Closing the Document 1 window	Avoiding splitting the screen	Switching between upper- and lowercase
When you want to close the Document 1 window rather than the Document 2 window, follow steps 1 through 3 on page 80, substituting appropriate document numbers. ◆	You don't have to split the Editing screen to have two documents active at the same time. Simply press Shift-F3 (Switch), and WordPerfect opens a Document 2 Editing screen. You can then retrieve a document into that screen and work with it as usual. You can switch between the screens by pressing Shift-F3 (Switch). ◆	Shift-F3 (Switch) can also be used to convert existing text to all uppercase or all lowercase letters. (For example, the word *all* can be converted to *ALL* and vice versa.) To convert case using Shift-F3 (Switch): **1.** Press Alt-F4 (Block), and block the desired text. **2.** Press Shift-F3 (Switch), and select 1 (Uppercase) or 2 (Lowercase). ◆

1. To create a new directory, press **F5** (List), and press **Enter** to display the List Files screen. Then select **7** (**O**ther Directory) from the List Files menu, type the full pathname of the new directory using eight characters or less for the actual directory name (*c:\wp51\lh*, for this example), press **Enter**, and select **Y**(es) to create the directory.

2. Next, move the highlight to the LH1.TEM file, and select **3** (**M**ove/Rename) from the List Files menu.

3. At the *New name* prompt, type *c:\wp51\lh\lh1.tem*, which is the complete pathname of the file in its new directory. (Alternatively, you can move the cursor to *FILES* in the pathname, delete *FILES*, and type *lh*.) Then press **Enter**. WordPerfect instantly moves the file to its new location.

4. Repeat steps 2 and 3 above to move the LH2.TEM file to the LH directory.

To be sure the LH1.TEM and LH2.TEM files really were moved to the new directory, follow these steps:

Viewing files in another directory

1. Move the highlight to Parent <Dir> (for parent directory, which in this case is the main WordPerfect directory, WP51) at the top of the List Files screen, and press **Enter** twice. The files and directories of WP51 are displayed in the List Files screen.

2. Move the highlight to LH <Dir> (for LH directory), and press **Enter** twice. The two letterhead files are now displayed in the List Files screen of the LH directory.

3. To return to the FILES directory, you must first return to the parent directory (WP51). With the highlight on Parent <Dir>, press **Enter** twice. Then move the highlight to FILES <Dir>, and press **Enter** twice.

That's all there is to it. Now you can create directories to organize all your WordPerfect documents.

On the facing page, you see a few other examples of letterheads that you can create in WordPerfect. By the time you finish reading this book, you will be able to figure out for yourself how to copy these examples or generate your own snazzy letterhead.

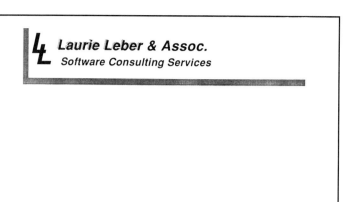

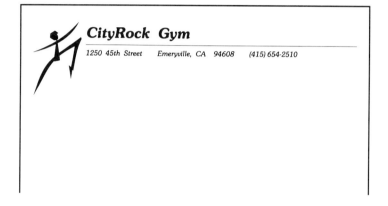

We've now covered the information you need to know to create two common types of business documents: memos and letters. In the next chapter, we show you how to create the elements often included in reports.

5

Professional Reports

Setting column widths
Page 113

Setting up tables
Page 108

Decimal alignment
Page 114

anging indents
Page 95

Suppressing headers
Page 119

Percent Change			
Drug	Adrenalin/Cocaine	Qnifen	Fiszol
Blood Pressure	250.6	25.78	2.3
Heart Rate	5.78	2.7	-3.67
Brain Stimulation	12.0	-34.28	2.46
Bone Structure	0	520.8	489.2
Risk of Stroke	2.7	1.56	0.91

Fox & Associates

Drug-Induced Stroke

produce damage to blood vessels which weaken their walls and, in the case of arteries in the brain, may lead to stroke. The evidence for the way in which these drugs produce this effect is not clear, but it is thought that it occurs in the following steps:

1. With continual administration over long periods of time, the drug accumulates in the cells that line the artery.

2. As the drug accumulates, it gradually inhibits the processes.

3. Eventually, the cells of the artery die, leaving the ve and vulnerable.

Qnifen and Fiszol: Both of these drugs are used to tre bone). Both have also been associated with stroke, but to var drugs is given below:

Qnifen was the first drug developed for use in osteoporosis. However, after several years of use, it became associated with stroke.

Fiszol wa treatmen Fiszol h Qnifen, will no Howev corrob

Although both Qnifen and Fiszol appear to be equally differ greatly in their chemical structures. While Qnifen has none. This structural difference may explain why incidence of stroke than patients taking Fiszol. The fol in the *New World Journal of Medicine*:

Fiszol would appear at this time to be a better of osteoporosis, because of the early reports with Fiszol.[1]

The following table compares the effects of adrenali as blood pressure, heart rate, and risk of stroke.

[1]R. Urban, "Fiszol versus Qnifen and Stroke," 1991.

DRUG-INDUCED STROKE

Risk Factors

A number of important health conditions are now recognized as contributing to the cause of stroke in humans. These include:

Age: The incidence of stroke increases dramatically with age. The chances of stroke are very small in young individuals. A sharp increase in the risk of stroke occurs in the population beyond 50 years of age.

Hypertension: The risk of stroke increases as does that of heart disease in humans who have elevated blood pressure. It has now been demonstrated by clinical trials that control of blood pressure is a major factor in reducing the incidence of stroke. Furthermore, the sooner increased blood pressure is diagnosed and treated, the greater the reduction of stroke as well as heart attack.

Smoking: Smoking is a well established risk for stroke. The longer an individual has smoked and the more they have smoked, the higher the risk of stroke as well as heart attack. It is now known that cessation of smoking at any time despite the duration of smoking will significantly reduce the risk of coronary disease and heart attack. Whether the same is true for stroke has yet to be demonstrated, but in all likelihood the same will apply.

Diabetes: Diabetes and some other chronic illnesses are associated with an increase in the incidence of stroke. Diabetics who do not have the other risk factors listed above are less likely to suffer stroke. Whether strict control of diabetes itself (maintaining as normal a blood sugar level as possible) reduces the risk of stroke is unknown at this time, but long-range clinical studies are in progress.

Drugs

Three classes of drugs used therapeutically or abused by drug-dependent individuals are associated with stroke.

Drugs That Stimulate Blood Pressure: This first class of drugs includes adrenalin, amphetamines, and cocaine. Adrenalin is used therapeutically to raise blood pressure while amphetamines and cocaine are commonly abused for their stimulatory effects. The principal actions of all these drugs are:

- Increase blood pressure
- Increase heart rate
- Stimulate brain

Drugs That Damage Blood Vessels: A few drugs used for long periods of time can

1

Making bullets
Page 100

Setting tabs
Page 97

In many professions, writing reports is a daily task. Whether you're a scientist, an administrative assistant, a marketing specialist, or an attorney, WordPerfect can help take the drudgery out of report writing. In this chapter, we'll introduce you to WordPerfect features for creating outlines, lists, footnotes, parallel columns, and tables. In addition, we'll show you how to add headers and numbers to your pages.

To demonstrate all these features, we need to work with a document that is longer than those we created in previous chapters. You can either create a report of your own or you can use the one shown on the previous page. In the following exercises, you type just enough text to use the feature we are discussing. You can refer to the report on the previous page to see how all these features can be combined to create a useful report.

Outlining a Document

Different people work in different ways. Some people launch right into a project, starting at the beginning and working their way through in a linear fashion until they've crossed the last *t* and dotted the last *i*. Others depend heavily on outlines, creating an overview of the project and then filling in the details. If you fall into the latter category, this section is for you. Although the report we're writing is relatively short, it contains enough headings to give you a good idea of how WordPerfect's Outline feature works.

The Outline feature allows you to have up to eight levels, each with a unique identification scheme, known collectively as *paragraph numbers*. Follow these steps to see how easy it is to create an outline in WordPerfect:

Creating an outline

1. Start with a clean WordPerfect screen (be sure the cursor is at the top of the screen).
2. Press **Shift-F5** (Date/Outline), select **4** (Outline), and then select **1** (**On**). The word *Outline* appears in the bottom-left corner of the screen.
3. Press **Enter** to start the outline. WordPerfect inserts a Roman numeral I at the top of the Editing screen.
4. Press **Alt-F3** (Reveal Codes). In the Reveal Codes screen, notice that WordPerfect has inserted an Outline

On code ([Outline On]) and an Automatic Paragraph Number code ([Par Num:Auto]). Every time you press Enter while Outline is turned on, WordPerfect inserts an Automatic Paragraph Number code after the hard return to designate a new outline level. Press **Alt-F3** (Reveal Codes) to return to the Editing screen.

Now enter the headings of the outline, using the Backspace or Del keys if you make a mistake:

1. Press **F4** (♦Indent) to indent the text you'll be typing after I. (Don't press the Tab key which, as you'll see in a minute, is used to change the outline level.)

2. Press the **Caps Lock** key, type *DRUG-INDUCED STROKE*, and then press **Enter** to start a new heading. WordPerfect inserts II at the beginning of the line.

3. Press the **Tab** key to change to level two. The cursor moves over one tab, and A replaces II. Press **F4** (♦Indent), type *Risk Factors*, and press **Enter** to start a new line. WordPerfect inserts B at the beginning of the line.

4. Press **Tab** to change to level three. The cursor moves over one more tab, and 1 replaces B. Press **F4** (♦Indent), type *Age*, and press **Enter** to start a new line. Word-Perfect inserts 2 at the beginning of the line.

5. Repeat the previous step for the headings *Hypertension*, *Smoking*, and *Diabetes*, pressing **Enter** after the last one.

6. Press **Shift-Tab** to change from level three to level two. The cursor moves back one tab, and the paragraph number B replaces 5. Press **F4** (♦Indent), type *Drugs*, and press **Enter** to start a new line.

7. Press **Tab** to change to level three. Press **F4** (♦Indent), type *Drugs That Stimulate Blood Pressure*, and press **Enter** to start a new line.

8. Repeat the previous step for the headings *Drugs That Damage Blood Vessels* and *Qnifen and Fiszol*, but don't press Enter after *Fiszol*.

9. Press **Shift-F5** (Date/Outline), and select **4** (**Outline**) and **2** (**Off**). WordPerfect inserts an Outline Off code into the document.

Changing outline levels

When you've completed the outline, it looks like this:

```
I.    DRUG-INDUCED STROKE
      A.    Risk Factors
            1.    Age
            2.    Hypertension
            3.    Smoking
            4.    Diabetes
      B.    Drugs
            1.    Drugs That Stimulate Blood Pressure
            2.    Drugs That Damage Blood Vessels
            3.    Qnifen and Fiszol
_




                                              Doc 1 Pg 1 Ln 2.83" Pos 1"
```

Press **F10** (Save) to save the outline with the filename
stroke.rpt, and then press **Shift-F7** (Print) and select **1** (Full
Document) to print the outline.

Filling In the Outline

You can use the outline you just created as a starting point
for the actual report. All you have to do is remove the Outline
On and Off codes and the Tab and Automatic Paragraph
Number codes, which will give you a chance to use the
Search and Replace features discussed in Chapter 3. To
remove these codes, follow these steps:

1. Press **Alt-F3** (Reveal Codes), move the cursor in the
    Reveal Codes screen to the Outline On code, and then
    press the **Del** key. WordPerfect simultaneously deletes
    the Outline Off code.

2. Next, delete the Hard Return code ([HRt]) at the top of
    the outline.

*Using Replace to
delete codes*

3. Use the Replace feature to delete the Tab codes. With
    the Reveal Codes screen still displayed, press **Alt-F2**
    (Replace), and when the *w/Confirm?* prompt appears,
    select **N**(o). Press the **Tab** key, and then press **F2**
    (▶Search) to have WordPerfect search on the Tab code
    [Tab]. At the *Replace with* prompt, simply press **F2**
    (▶Search) so that WordPerfect replaces the Tab codes

with nothing. The *Please wait* message is displayed as WordPerfect deletes the Tab codes from the outline.

4. Next, replace the Automatic Paragraph Number codes with nothing. Press **Home,Home,Up Arrow**, press **Alt-F2** (Replace), and select **N**(o). Press **Shift-F5** (Date/Outline), select **2** (**P**ara Num), and press **F2** (◆Search). Finally, at the *Replace with* prompt, press **F2** (◆Search).

5. Now for the Indent codes, some of which you want to delete and some of which you want to replace with tabs. Press **Home,Home,Up Arrow**, and delete the Indent code preceding the *DRUG-INDUCED STROKE* heading. Delete the Indent codes preceding the *Risk Factors* and *Drugs* headings. Then press **Alt-F3** (Reveal Codes) to return to the Editing screen.

6. To replace the remaining Indent codes with tabs, start by pressing **Home,Home,Up Arrow**. Then press **Alt-F2** (Replace), and select **N**(o). Press **F4** (◆Indent), and then press **F2** (◆Search) to have WordPerfect search on the Indent code. Press the **Tab** key, and then press **F2** (◆Search) again to have WordPerfect substitute Tab codes for the remaining Indent codes.

The *STROKE.RPT* document now looks like this:

```
DRUG-INDUCED STROKE
Risk Factors
      Age
      Hypertension
      Smoking
      Diabetes
Drugs
      Drugs That Stimulate Blood Pressure
      Drugs That Damage Blood Vessels
      Qnifen and Fiszol




















C:\WP51\FILES\STROKE.RPT                    Doc 1 Pg 1 Ln 1" Pos 1"
```

Now you're ready to start entering and formatting the text of the report.

1. Press **Home,Home,Up Arrow**, and then press **Shift-F6** (Center) to center the *DRUG-INDUCED STROKE* heading.

2. Block the heading, press **F6** (Bold) to make the heading bold, and then add two blank lines between this heading and the next one.

3. Repeat the previous step for the *Risk Factors* and *Drugs* headings, adding only one blank line after each heading.

4. Move the cursor to the *Risk Factors* heading, and press the **Down Arrow** key twice. Type the following:

   A number of important health conditions are now recognized as contributing to the cause of stroke in humans. These include:

5. Press **Enter** once to add a blank line below the text.

6. Move the cursor to the *Drugs* heading, and press the **Down Arrow** key twice. Type the following:

   Three classes of drugs used therapeutically or abused by drug-dependent individuals are associated with stroke.

7. Press **Enter** once to add a blank line.

Before you move on to the next section, type a colon followed by a space after each of the seven level-three headings, and then press **F10** (Save) to save the *STROKE.RPT* document.

Changing numbering style

To change the numbering style used in the outline: **1.** Press Shift-F5 (Date/Outline), and select 6 (Define). The Paragraph Number Definition menu appears, displaying five numbering styles—Paragraph, Outline, Legal, Bullets, and User-defined (used to create your own numbering style). **2.** Using the examples given on the menu as a guide, select the number corresponding to the style you want. **3.** Press F7 (Exit) twice to return to the Editing screen. If you're changing the style of an existing outline, you must be sure the cursor is at the beginning of the outline before you press Shift-F5 (Date/Outline), and when you return to the Editing screen, you must press Home, Down Arrow to reformat the outline. ♦

Changing levels

To change the level of an existing outline heading, in the Reveal Codes screen place the cursor to the right of the Automatic Paragraph Number code of the heading you want to change, and then press Tab (for the next level) or Shift-Tab (for the previous level). ♦

Automating Tasks with Macros

In the course of carrying out your work, you will often find yourself repeating the same task over and over again. For example, you might have to repeatedly type the same name or phrase, or you might need to format a series of headings with the same attributes. For times like these, WordPerfect's Macro feature comes in handy.

WordPerfect *macros* are scripts, or small programs, that automate tasks normally accomplished with a series of keystrokes. You can create macros that perform all sorts of tasks—from saving and printing a file to typing a letterhead. You simply give the macro a name, "record" the keystrokes that you want the macro to duplicate, and then "play back" the macro when you want WordPerfect to perform that particular task.

Increasing efficiency with macros

We don't intend to go into great detail about the capabilities of the Macro feature in this section, but we do want to point out that, with a little imagination, you can use macros to take the drudgery out of text entry and formatting.

A Text-Entry Macro

Let's create a simple macro that types the word *stroke* every time you press two keys:

1. Place the cursor in the *Age:* heading, and press the **End** key to move to the end of the line.

Naming macros	Starting over	Editing macros
In WordPerfect, you can name macros in three ways: by entering up to eight characters; by holding down the Alt key and typing a single letter from A to Z; or by pressing Enter. ♦	If you make a mistake while defining a macro and want to start over, press Ctrl-F10 (Macro Define) to stop recording keystrokes, then press Ctrl-F10 (Macro Define) again, enter the same name, and select 1 (Replace) from the menu at the bottom of the screen. Select Y(es) to replace the existing macro file, and press Enter. You can then redefine the macro. ♦	To edit an existing macro, press Ctrl-F10 (Macro Define), enter the macro name, and select 2 (Edit). The Macro Editor appears, displaying the macro, which you can then edit by inserting or deleting text, keystroke commands, and macro commands (press Ctrl-PgUp to display a list of macro commands). ♦

2. Press **Ctrl-F10** (Macro Define). The *Define macro* prompt appears in the bottom-left corner of the screen.
3. Press **Alt-S** for the macro name, and then press **Enter**.
4. At the *Description* prompt, type *stroke*, and press **Enter**.
5. When the *Macro Def* prompt appears, type *stroke*. The word *stroke* is displayed on the screen as you type, allowing you to make any corrections before you finish defining the macro.
6. Press **Ctrl-F10** (Macro Define) to end the macro definition.

Now play back, or run, the macro:

Running macros

1. Press **Ctrl-Backspace** (Delete Word) to delete the word *stroke* in the Editing screen, and type the following:

   The incidence of

2. Next, type a space, and press **Alt-S**. WordPerfect instantly inserts the word *stroke*.
3. Type another space, and continue the paragraph as follows, pressing **Alt-S** when you want to insert the word *stroke*:

   increases dramatically with age. The chances of stroke *are very small in young individuals. A sharp increase in the risk of* stroke *occurs in the population beyond 50 years of age.*

   Press **Enter** once to add some space. This is the result:

```
                    DRUG-INDUCED STROKE


Risk Factors

A number of important health conditions are now recognized as
contributing to the cause of stroke in humans. These include:

     Age: The incidence of stroke increases dramatically with age.
The chances of stroke are very small in young individuals. A sharp
increase in the risk of stroke occurs in the population beyond 50
years of age.
  -
     Hypertension:
     Smoking:
     Diabetes:
Drugs

Three classes of drugs used therapeutically or abused by drug-
dependent individuals are associated with stroke.

     Drugs That Stimulate Blood Pressure:
     Drugs That Damage Blood Vessels:
     Qnifen and Fiszol:
C:\WP51\FILES\STROKE.RPT                      Doc 1 Pg 1 Ln 3" Pos 1"
```

Now all you have to do to insert the word *stroke* anywhere in the report is to repeat step 2 above. This may seem like a trivial example, but imagine the impact on your efficiency if the report included 20 instances of *acetylcholinesterase* or *Rebecca Brand v. Midvalley Clinic*, instead of 20 instances of *stroke*. Enter the following paragraphs after the *Hypertension:*, *Smoking:*, and *Diabetes:* headings to get an idea of the time you can save. Press **Enter** once after each paragraph.

Hypertension: *The risk of* stroke *increases as does that of heart disease in humans who have elevated blood pressure. It has now been demonstrated by clinical trials that control of blood pressure is a major factor in reducing the incidence of* stroke. *Furthermore, the sooner increased blood pressure is diagnosed and treated, the greater the reduction of* stroke *as well as heart attack.*

Smoking: *Smoking is a well established risk for* stroke. *The longer an individual has smoked and the more they have smoked, the higher the risk of* stroke *as well as heart attack. It is now known that cessation of smoking at any time despite the duration of smoking will significantly reduce the risk of coronary disease and heart attack. Whether the same is true for* stroke *has yet to be demonstrated, but in all likelihood the same will apply.*

Diabetes: *Diabetes and some other chronic illnesses are associated with an increase in the incidence of* stroke. *Diabetics who do not have the other risk factors*

Macro descriptions

Macro descriptions can be up to 39 characters and are optional. They can be viewed only in the Macro Editor, which you activate by pressing Ctrl-F10 (Macro Define), entering the macro name, and selecting 3 (Description). The *Description* prompt appears, displaying the description. You can then edit or delete the description (or accept it as is by pressing Enter). ◆

Reusable macros

When you create a macro, WordPerfect automatically saves the macro file with a .WPM extension. The macro can then be used in any WordPerfect document. You can delete a macro file, like any other WordPerfect file, by highlighting it in the List Files screen, and pressing 2 (Delete). ◆

Macro directory

Macro files are stored in the main WordPerfect directory (C:\WP51). You can change the directory where macro files are stored by pressing Shift-F1 (Setup), selecting 6 (Location of Files) and 2 (Keyboard/Macro File), typing the pathname of the directory where you want the files to be stored (for example, *c:\wp51\files*), and then pressing Enter. ◆

listed above are less likely to suffer stroke. *Whether strict control of diabetes itself (maintaining as normal a blood sugar level as possible) reduces the risk of* stroke *is unknown at this time, but long-range clinical studies are in progress.*

A Text-Formatting Macro

For our second example, we'll show you how to create a macro that underlines headings:

1. Place the cursor at the beginning of the first level-three heading, *Age:*.
2. Press **Ctrl-F10** (Macro Define), and at the *Define macro* prompt, type *u* for the macro name, press **Enter**, type *Underline* as the description, and press **Enter**.
3. When the *Macro Def* prompt appears, press **Alt-F4** (Block), and type a colon to block the entire heading (including the colon). Then press **F8** (Underline) to underline the heading.
4. Press **Ctrl-F10** (Macro Define) to end the macro definition.

Now play back, or run, the macro:

1. Place the cursor at the beginning of *Hypertension: .*
2. Press **Alt-F10** (Macro), type *u*, and press **Enter**.
3. Repeat these steps for the other level-three headings.

The report now looks like this:

```
     Smoking: Smoking is a well-established risk for stroke. The
longer an individual has smoked and the more they have smoked, the
higher the risk of stroke as well as heart attack. It is now known
that cessation of smoking at any time despite the duration of
smoking will significantly reduce the risk of coronary disease and
heart attack. Whether the same is true for stroke has yet to be
demonstrated, but in all likelihood the same will apply.

     Diabetes: Diabetes and some other chronic illnesses are
associated with an increase in the incidence of stroke. Diabetics
who do not have the other risk factors listed above are less likely
to suffer stroke. Whether strict control of diabetes itself
(maintaining as normal a blood sugar level as possible) reduces the
risk of stroke is unknown at this time, but long-range clinical
studies are in progress.

Drugs

Three classes of drugs used therapeutically or abused by drug-
dependent individuals are associated with stroke.

     Drugs That Stimulate Blood Pressure:
     Drugs That Damage Blood Vessels:
     Qnifen and Fiszol:
C:\WP51\FILES\STROKE.RPT                          Doc 1 Pg 1 Ln 8.33" Pos 3.3"
```

Save the report by pressing **F10** (Save).

Creating Lists

In Chapter 3, you created a numbered list in the example letter by simply indenting lines using the Tab key. This method worked because the list was very straightforward, and each item in the list was only one line long. In this section, we'll show you how to format lists with items more than one line long, and we'll show you how to use special characters to create professional-looking bulleted lists. In the process, you'll learn how to set custom tabs for those times when WordPerfect's default tabs don't meet your needs.

Numbered Lists

The example report contains a numbered list under the heading *Drugs That Damage Blood Vessels:*. Generally, you use numbered lists for step-by-step instructions or sequential processes. We'll use this example to show you how to create a *hanging indent*, like the ones used for the instructions in this book. We'll use the Tab key to indent the items and to insert a fixed amount of space between each item's number (in this case, 1, 2, and 3) and its text, and we'll see how to set custom tabs.

Hanging indents

Start by typing the text of the numbered list:

1. Locate the *Drugs That Damage Blood Vessels:* heading, and press the **End** key to move to the end of the line.

2. Type the following (remember to press **Alt-S** to insert the word *stroke*):

    A few drugs used for long periods of time can produce damage to blood vessels which weaken their walls and, in the case of arteries in the brain, may lead to stroke. *The evidence for the way in which these drugs produce this effect is not clear, but it is thought that it occurs in the following steps:*

3. Press **Enter** twice to create a blank line and start the first numbered item.

4. Press **Tab** to move over one tab. Press **Shift-F4** (♦Indent♦) and **Shift-Tab** to create a hanging indent. Type *1.*, press **Tab** to move over another tab, and type

With continual administration over long periods of time, the drug accumulates in the cells that line the artery.

Then press **Enter** twice to start the second numbered item. (Don't be alarmed if WordPerfect inserts a soft page break at this point; the position of the page break will change as you edit the text.)

5. Press **Tab**, and then press **Shift-F4** (◆Indent◆) and **Shift-Tab**. Type *2.*, press Tab again, type

As the drug accumulates, it gradually inhibits the cells' metabolic processes.

and then press **Enter** twice.

6. Press **Tab**, and then press **Shift-F4** (◆Indent◆) and **Shift-Tab**. Type *3.*, press **Tab** again, and type

Eventually, the cells of the artery die, leaving the vessel wall weakened and vulnerable.

Press **Enter** just once this time.

The numbered list now looks like this:

```
dependent individuals are associated with stroke.

     Drugs That Stimulate Blood Pressure:
     Drugs That Damage Blood Vessels: A few drugs used for long
periods of time can produce damage to blood vessels which weaken
their walls and in the case of arteries in the brain, may lead to
stroke. The evidence for the way in which these drugs produce this
effect is not clear, but it is thought that it occurs in the
following steps:

     1.   With continual administration over long
          periods of time, the drug accumulates in the
          cells that line the artery.
     ----------------------------------------------------------------
     2.   As the drug accumulates, it gradually inhibits
          the cells metabolic processes.

     3.   Eventually, the cells of the artery die,
          leaving the vessel wall weakened and
          vulnerable.
 _
     Qnifen and Fiszol:

C:\WP51\FILES\STROKE.RPT                          Doc 1 Pg 2 Ln 2" Pos 1"
```

So far, so good. But notice that using the default tab settings produce a rather large space between the numbers and their corresponding text. Let's tighten up the spacing a bit by setting custom tabs at the beginning of the list. Follow these steps:

1. Place the cursor anywhere on the last line of the paragraph that precedes the numbered list, and press the **End** key to move to the end of the line.

2. Press **Shift-F8** (Format), select **1** (**L**ine), and then select **8** (**T**ab Set).

3. When WordPerfect displays the Tab Set menu, press **Home,Home,Left Arrow** to move to the beginning of the Tab Set line, and then press **Ctrl-End** (Delete EOL) to delete all the current tab settings.

4. To set two tabs, one at 0.5 inch and the other at 0.8 inch, simply type *0.5* and press **Enter**, and then type *0.8* and press **Enter**. (When you're entering tab settings that are less than one inch, they must always be preceded by a zero.)

5. Press **F7** (Exit) twice to return to the Editing screen.

Setting tabs

Here's the result:

```
dependent individuals are associated with stroke.

   Drugs That Stimulate Blood Pressure:
   Drugs That Damage Blood Vessels: A few drugs used for long
periods of time can produce damage to blood vessels which weaken
their walls and in the case of arteries in the brain, may lead to
stroke. The evidence for the way in which these drugs produce this
effect is not clear, but it is thought that it occurs in the
following steps:_

     1. With continual administration over long periods of
        time, the drug accumulates in the cells that line
        the artery.

--------------------------------------------------------------------
     2. As the drug accumulates, it gradually inhibits the
        cells metabolic processes.

     3. Eventually, the cells of the artery die, leaving
        the vessel wall weakened and vulnerable.

   Qnifen and Fiszol:

C:\WP51\FILES\STROKE.RPT                    Doc 1 Pg 1 Ln 9" Pos 2.6"
```

Now you must return the tabs to their default settings after the numbered list so that the custom tab settings don't affect the rest of the report.

1. Place the cursor on the last line of the third numbered item, and press the End key to move to the end of the numbered list.

2. Press **Shift-F8** (Format), and then select **1** (**L**ine) and **8** (**T**ab Set).

3. Press **Home,Home,Left Arrow**, and then press **Ctrl-End** (Delete EOL) to delete the custom tab settings.

Returning to default tab settings

4. Type *0,.5* (yes, you do have to type the comma after the zero), and press **Enter** to reset the default tab settings.

5. Press **F7** (Exit) twice to return to the Editing screen.

Save the report without clearing the screen by pressing **F10** (Save).

Bulleted Lists

If you look back at the report shown at the beginning of the chapter, you'll see a bulleted list near the bottom of the first page. Generally, you use bullets for lists of items that are not sequential or hierarchical. In this example, we'll first use asterisks (*) as bullets; then we'll show you how to create real bullets with WordPerfect's Compose feature.

As with the numbered list in the previous exercise, we'll set some custom tabs. (If the items in your bulleted list are more than one line, you can create a hanging indent like the one in the numbered list.) Start by typing the text of the list:

1. Locate the *Drugs That Stimulate Blood Pressure:* heading, and press the **End** key to move to the end of the line.

2. Type the following:

   This first class of drugs includes adrenalin, amphetamines, and cocaine. Adrenalin is used therapeutically to raise blood pressure while amphetamines and cocaine are commonly abused for their stimulatory effects. The principal actions of all these drugs are:

3. To set the custom tabs, press **Shift-F8** (Format), select **1** (Line), and then select **8** (Tab Set). Then press **Home,Home,Left Arrow** to move to the beginning of the Tab Set line, press **Ctrl-End** (Delete EOL) to delete all the current tab settings, type *0.5*, press **Enter**, type *0.8*, press **Enter**, and finally, press **F7** (Exit) twice to return to the Editing screen.

4. Press **Enter** twice to create a blank line and start the first bulleted item. Then press **Tab** to move over one tab, type *, press **Tab** again to move over another tab, type *Increase blood pressure*, and then press **Enter** once to start the second bulleted item.

5. Press **Tab**, type *, press Tab again, type *Increase heart rate*, and then press **Enter** once.

6. Press **Tab**, type *, press Tab again, type *Stimulate brain*, and press **Enter** once.

Now return the tab settings to their default settings:

1. Press **Shift-F8** (Format), and then select **1** (**L**ine) and **8** (**T**ab Set).

2. To reset the tab settings to their defaults, simply press **Home,Home,Left Arrow**, press **Ctrl-End** (Delete EOL) to delete the custom tab settings, type *0,.5*, and press **Enter**.

3. Press **F7** (Exit) twice to return to the Editing screen.

The bulleted list looks like this:

```
dependent individuals are associated with stroke.

     Drugs That Stimulate Blood Pressure: This first class of drugs
includes adrenalin, amphetamines, and cocaine. Adrenalin is used
therapeutically to raise blood pressure while amphetamines and
cocaine are commonly abused for their stimulatory effects. The
principal actions of these drugs are:

     *  Increase blood pressure
     *  Increase heart rate
     *  Stimulate brain
 _
     Drugs That Damage Blood Vessels: A few drugs used for long
periods of time can produce damage to blood vessels which weaken
------------------------------------------------------------------------
their walls and in the case of arteries in the brain, may lead to
stroke. The evidence for the way in which these drugs produce this
effect is not clear, but it is thought that it occurs in the
following steps:

     1. With continual administration over long periods of
        time, the drug accumulates in the cells that line
        the artery.

C:\WP51\FILES\STROKE.RPT                    Doc 1 Pg 1 Ln 9.5" Pos 1"
```

Save the report without clearing the screen by pressing **F10** (Save).

Inserting bullet characters   Aside from the characters you see on your keyboard, WordPerfect can create a number of *special* characters, including math symbols, Greek characters, and letters with foreign accent marks. To insert a special character, you turn on WordPerfect's Compose feature by pressing Ctrl-2 (Compose) and then pressing the key or key combination that inserts the character you want. Some characters in the WordPerfect character sets don't appear in the Editing screen, but you can see them in the View Document

Math symbols and Greek characters

Making bullets

screen. (Depending on your printer's capabilities, you might not be able to print all the available characters.)

A few of the characters available for use as bullets are •, °, and o. For this example, we'll use a medium-sized filled bullet, like the one used in the report shown at the beginning of the chapter. Follow these steps:

1. Place the cursor on the asterisk preceding the first bulleted item, and press **Del** to delete the asterisk.
2. To insert a medium-sized filled bullet at the cursor, press **Ctrl-2** (Compose), and type *4,0*. (You specify the bullet by typing the character-set number—in this case 4—followed by a comma and the character number— in this case 0.) Then press **Enter**. WordPerfect inserts a medium-sized filled bullet.
3. Repeat the previous steps to replace the asterisks preceding the second and third bulleted items.
4. To see the character-set numbers, press **Alt-F3** (Reveal Codes), and move the cursor in the Reveal Codes screen to the bullet character. Press **Alt-F3** (Reveal Codes) to return to the Editing screen.

Save the report without clearing the screen by pressing **F10** (Save).

WordPerfect characters

For a complete list of all the characters available with WordPerfect's Compose feature, see Appendix P: "WordPerfect Characters" in the *WordPerfect Reference Manual*. ♦

Bullet characters

You can press Ctrl-2 (Compose), and use asterisks in conjunction with other keys to create a variety of bullets. Here are the keystrokes:

Ctrl-2,*,. (period)   .
Ctrl-2,*,*   •
Ctrl-2,*,o   ○
Ctrl-2,*,O   o ♦

More about Compose

To use the Compose feature, be sure to press Ctrl-2 (Compose) and not Ctrl-F2 (Spell).

You can also press Ctrl-v (rather than Ctrl-2) to turn on the Compose feature. If you press Ctrl-v, the prompt *Key* = appears. You can then enter the desired character-set and character numbers (as we describe in step 2 above). ♦

Adding Footnotes

Some reports are more likely to have footnotes than others. If you use information from outside sources or want to steer readers toward data that backs up your arguments, you'll probably want to give credit or bibliographic information in footnotes, rather than cluttering up the body of the report. In this section, we show you how to create the footnote that you can see on page two of the example report at the beginning of the chapter.

This footnote occurs in a paragraph following the *Qnifen and Fiszol:* heading, so start by typing the text:

1. Place the cursor in the *Qnifen and Fiszol:* heading, press the **End** key to move to the end of the line, and then press **Enter** twice to start a new paragraph.

2. Type the following, using the stroke macro where appropriate:

    Although both Qnifen and Fiszol appear to be equally effective in treating osteoporosis, they differ greatly in their chemical structures. While Qnifen contains one methyl group (CH3), Fiszol has none. This structural difference may explain why patients taking Qnifen have a higher incidence of stroke *than patients taking Fiszol. The following statement was recently published in the New World Journal of Medicine:*

3. If you want, italicize the name of the journal, and then press **Enter** twice to start a new line.

4. Press **Shift-F4** (◆Indent◆) to indent the next paragraph—a quotation—from both the left and right margins. The cursor moves to the first tab stop. Now, type the following:

    Fiszol would appear at this time to be a better choice than Qnifen in the treatment of osteoporosis, because of the early reports of fewer cases of stroke *associated with Fiszol.*

Double indenting

Check the results in the View Document screen, shown here:

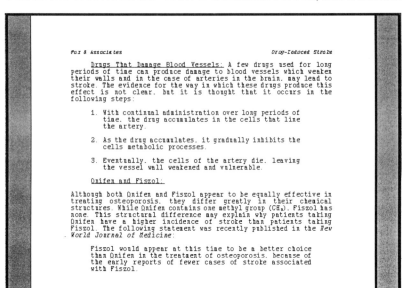

Save the report without clearing the screen by pressing **F10** (Save). Then we'll create the footnote:

1. Be sure the cursor is located on the space after the period in the quotation.

2. Press **Ctrl-F7** (Footnote), select **1** (Footnote), and then select **1** (Create). A special Note Editing screen appears with the number of this footnote in the top-left corner and the type of note (Footnote or Endnote) in the bottom-left corner, as shown on the following page.

Subscript

To subscript a character: **1.** Block the character (for example, the 3 in *CH3*). **2.** Press Ctrl-F8 (Font), and select 1 (Size) and 2 (Subscpt).

To decrease the size of the subscript (for the sake of appearance), **1.** Reblock the character. **2.** Press Ctrl-F8 (Font), and select 1 (Size) and 4 (Small) . ◆

Entering footnotes

A footnote can contain approximately 65,000 characters. You can type the text of the footnote in the Note Editing screen just as you would type text in the normal Editing screen, using such features as Bold, Italic, Block, Move, and so on. You can also use the Speller. ◆

Setting off footnotes

By default, WordPerfect inserts a 2-inch line between a footnote and the text. To change to no line at all or to a margin-to-margin line: **1.** Press Ctrl-F7 (Footnote), and select 1 (Footnote) and 4 (Options). **2.** Select 7 (Line Separating Text and Footnotes), and then select 1 (No Line) or 3 (Margin to Margin). **3.** Press F7 (Exit) to return to the Editing screen. ◆

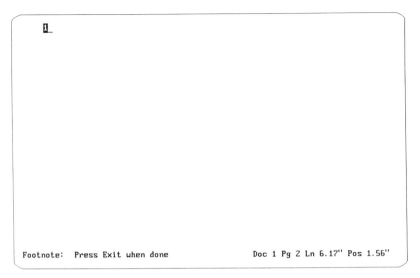

3. Type the following in the Note Editing screen:

   R. Urban, "Fiszol versus Qnifen and Stroke." New World Journal of Medicine, 217: 312-315, 1991.

4. Press **F7** (Exit) to save the footnote and return to the Editing screen. WordPerfect has inserted a highlighted number 1 after the quotation. You can't see the footnote in the Editing screen, but you can see it in the View Document screen, as shown here:

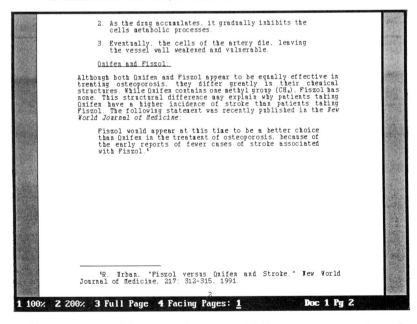

You can use this procedure to add footnotes anywhere in your document. For each footnote, WordPerfect inserts a Note code ([Footnote:#;[Note Num]*text*], where # is the footnote number, and *text* is the first 50 characters of foot-note text). If you insert a new footnote before an existing footnote, WordPerfect automatically renumbers the exist-ing footnote. For example, if you add a footnote to page one of the report, WordPerfect changes the number of the footnote you just created to 2. You can delete a footnote simply by deleting the Note code in the Reveal Codes screen or by deleting the footnote reference number in the Editing screen. When you delete a footnote, WordPerfect automatically renumbers the remaining footnotes.

*Deleting
footnotes*

Editing Footnotes

You can edit an existing footnote if you know its reference number. Follow the steps below to add formatting to the footnote you just created:

1. Press **Ctrl-F7** (Footnote), and select **1** (Footnote) and **2** (Edit).
2. WordPerfect prompts you for the reference number of the footnote you want to edit. Type *1*, and press **Enter**.
3. When WordPerfect displays the footnote in the Note Editing screen, block *New World Journal of Medicine*. Then press **Ctrl-F8** (Font), and select **2** (Appearance) and **4** (Italc) to make the journal name italic.
4. Next, block the number 217, and press **F8** (Underline) to add underlining.
5. Press **F7** (Exit) to save your changes and return to the Editing screen.

Save the report without clearing the screen by pressing **F10** (Save). You can check how the edited footnote looks in the View Document screen.

Footnote Placement

When you add a footnote to a document, WordPerfect places the footnote at the bottom of the page on which the reference number occurs and separates the footnote from the main text with a 2-inch line. If the footnote is too long to fit entirely on the page, WordPerfect tries to retain at least 1/2 inch of the footnote text on the same page as its reference number. If the footnote simply won't fit, WordPerfect breaks the page, moving both the text containing the reference number and the footnote to the next page.

You can tell WordPerfect to put endnotes at the end of a document instead of footnotes at the foot of a page by pressing Ctrl-F7 (Footnote) and selecting 2 (Endnote) instead of 1 (Footnote).

Endnotes

Using the Table Feature

In this section, we'll explore two ways to use WordPerfect's Table feature to format information so that it is readily accessible to your readers. First, we'll take a look at parallel columns, which allow you to present unequal columns of information side-by-side. Then we'll show you how to create traditional tables, complete with gridlines and borders.

Parallel Columns

Parallel columns, also called *side-by-side paragraphs,* are useful for creating documents such as inventory descriptions and presentation notes. The easiest way to understand this concept is to look at an example.

In the report shown at the beginning of the chapter, parallel columns are used in the middle of the second page to summarize the drugs Qnifen and Fiszol. You cannot use tabs or indents to create parallel columns; you must use Word-Perfect's Table feature. Start by writing a lead-in paragraph for the parallel-column format:

1. Place the cursor in the *Qnifen and Fiszol:* heading, press the **End** key to move to the end of the line.

2. Type the following, using the stroke macro:

   Both of these drugs are used to treat osteoporosis (softening of the bone). Both have also been associated with stroke, *but to varying degrees. A summary of the drugs is given below:*

3. Press **Enter** once to insert a blank line, and then press **Down Arrow** once to place the cursor on the second blank line below the paragraph you just typed.

Now set up the columns, as follows:

1. Press **Alt-F7** (Columns/Table), select **1** (Columns), and then select **3** (**D**efine). The Text Column Definition menu appears, as shown on the following page.

Setting up columns

```
Text Column Definition

    1 - Type                              Newspaper

    2 - Number of Columns                 2

    3 - Distance Between Columns

    4 - Margins

    Column   Left     Right    Column   Left     Right
      1:     1"       4"        13:
      2:     4.5"     7.5"      14:
      3:                        15:
      4:                        16:
      5:                        17:
      6:                        18:
      7:                        19:
      8:                        20:
      9:                        21:
     10:                        22:
     11:                        23:
     12:                        24:

Selection: 0
```

2. Select **1** (**T**ype) and **2** (**P**arallel). Accept the default setting of 2 for the Number of Columns option. (You can have up to 24 parallel columns.)

3. Select **4** (**M**argins), type *1.5* for the left margin of the first column, and press **Enter**. Then press **Down Arrow**, type *7.0* for the right margin of the second column, and press **Enter**.

4. Press **F7** (Exit), and select **1** (**O**n) from the menu at the bottom of the screen to turn on the Columns feature.

   Notice that the status line indicates a cursor position of 1.5. The left and right margins of the first column are 1.5 and 4.0 inches, and the left and right margins of the second column are 4.5 and 7.0 inches.

5. Before you enter the text for the columns, you need to insert a Column Off code ([Col Off]) after the Column On code ([Col On]). WordPerfect then knows that the rest of the report text is not part of the parallel column format. Without moving the cursor, press **Alt-F7** (Columns/ Table), and select **1** (Columns) and **2** (Off).

WordPerfect inserts a Hard Page code and a Column Off code. You can now place the cursor between the Column On and Off codes and type the text of the columns.

1. Press **Alt-F3** (Reveal Codes), and place the cursor on the Hard Page code ([HPg]). Press **Alt-F3** (Reveal Codes) to return to the Editing Screen, and then type the following text:

Qnifen was the first drug developed for use in osteo-porosis. However, after several years of use, it became associated with stroke.

2. Press **Ctrl-Enter** to move the cursor to the top of the second column, and type the following:

Fiszol was recently approved for the treatment of osteoporosis. Because Fiszol has a different structure from Qnifen, current theory is that Fiszol will not have the same side effects. However, clinical trials have not yet corroborated this theory.

The parallel columns look like this:

```
Qnifen and Fiszol: Both of these drugs are used to treat
osteoporosis (softening of the bone). Both have also been
associated with stroke, but to varying degrees. A summary of the
drugs is given below:

    Qnifen was the first drug       Fiszol was recently
    developed for use in            approved for treatment of
    osteoporosis. However,          osteoporosis. Because
    after several years of          Fiszol has a different
    use, it became associated       structure from Qnifen,
    with stroke.                    current theory is that
                                    Fiszol will not have the
                                    same side effects.
                                    However, clinical trials
                                    have not yet corroborated
                                    this theory. _

Although both Qnifen and Fiszol appear to be equally effective in
treating osteoporosis, they differ greatly in their chemical
structures. While Qnifen contains one methyl group (CH3), Fiszol has
none. This structural difference may explain why patients taking
Qnifen have a higher incidence of stroke than patients taking
```

Save the report by pressing **F10** (Save).

Moving the cursor in parallel columns

Navigating parallel columns is simple. You can move from one column to another by using Ctrl-Home (Go To) together with the Left Arrow and Right Arrow keys. Press Ctrl-Home,Left Arrow to move one column to the left, and Ctrl-Home,Right Arrow to move one column to the right. To move to the top or bottom of the current column, press Ctrl-Home,Up Arrow or Ctrl-Home,Down Arrow. If more than two parallel columns are on a page, press Ctrl-Home,Home,Left Arrow or Ctrl-Home,Home, Right Arrow to move to the first column or last column on the page. ◆

Newspaper columns

You can also create newspaper columns in Word-Perfect (where the text "snakes" from one column to the next). Simply select 1 (Newspaper) for the Type option on the Text Column Definition menu, and set the other options on the menu as desired. ◆

Traditional Tables

Tables are standard features of reports. Why then are tables so difficult to create in most word-processing programs? Not so with WordPerfect. You use the Table feature to specify the number of columns and rows and then leave it to WordPerfect to figure out the initial settings.

To demonstrate how easy the process is, we'll use the table from the example report. Start by adding a lead-in paragraph at the end of the report document:

1. Press **Home,Home,Down Arrow**, and press **Enter** twice to add a blank line and start a new line.

2. Type the following:

    The following table compares the effects of adrenalin/cocaine, Qnifen, and Fiszol on such factors as blood pressure, heart rate, and risk of stroke.

3. Press **Ctrl-Enter** to insert a hard page break so that the table can begin on page 3 of the report.

Now you can start assembling the table:

Setting up tables

1. Press **Alt-F7** (Columns/Table), and select **2** (**T**ables) and **1** (**C**reate).

2. When the prompt *Number of Columns* appears, type *4*, and press **Enter**.

3. When the prompt *Number of Rows* appears, type *6*, and press **Enter**.

This table, consisting of four columns and six rows, appears:

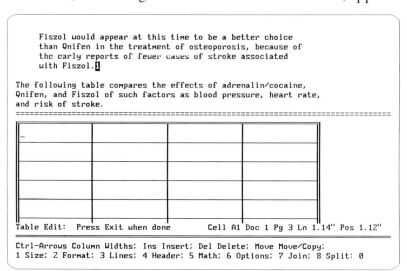

The Table Edit menu is also displayed, indicating that you're in the Table Editor. Here, you can change the structure and format of the table, but you cannot enter any data in it.

1. Press **F7** (Exit) to return to the normal Editing screen.

2. Now press **Alt-F3** (Reveal Codes). The Table Definition code ([Tbl Def]) and the Table Off code ([Tbl Off]) tell WordPerfect where the table begins and ends. The Row and Cell codes ([Row] and [Cell]) tell WordPerfect where the rows and cells begin and end.

3. Press **Alt-F3** (Reveal Codes) to return to the Editing screen.

Notice that a double border surrounds the table, and single borders divide the columns and rows into cells. *Cell A1* is displayed at the beginning of the status line, letting you know that the cursor is currently located in the cell at the intersection of the first column (column A) and the first row (row 1). Each cell in the table has a similar *address*, allowing you to quickly determine the position of the cursor by watching the status line. You enter data in the Editing screen, as follows:

1. To enter the column headings, type *Percent Change* in cell A1, and press **Tab** to move to cell B1. Type *Adrenalin/Cocaine*, and press **Tab** to move to cell C1. (You'll widen the column later to adjust the way *Cocaine* breaks.) Type *Fiszol*, and press **Tab** to move to cell D1. Finally, type *Qnifen*, and press **Tab** to move to cell A2.

Switching to the Table Editor

Before you can switch to the Table Editor from the normal Editing Screen, you must position the cursor within the table. ◆

Entering text in tables

When you add text to the table in the normal Editing screen, you can use most of WordPerfect's features, including appearance and size attributes, fonts, the Speller, and Footnote. ◆

Deleting tables

If you delete the Table Definition code, the Table Off, Row, and Cell codes are also deleted, and WordPerfect places tabs between the columns of the table (using the current tab settings). You cannot restore a deleted table with F1 (Cancel) unless the table and the Table Definition code were deleted at the same time. ◆

2. Finish the table by typing the entries shown below, pressing **Tab** to move from cell to cell. (Pressing Shift-Tab moves the cursor to the previous cell, and you can also use the Arrow keys to move around.)

Blood Pressure	*250.6*	*2.3*	*25.78*
Heart Rate	*5.78*	*-3.67*	*2.7*
Brain Stimulation	*12.0*	*2.466*	*-34.28*
Bone Structure	*0*	*489.2*	*520.8*
Risk of Stroke	*2.7*	*0.91*	*1.56*

Looking over the table, you can see one or two changes that would make it more effective. To make structural changes to the table, you must return to the Table Editor, so press **Alt-F7** (Columns/Table).

Rearranging the table   You can rearrange the rows and columns in a table with WordPerfect's Move feature. Using Move in the Table Editor is similar to using it in the Editing screen. Follow along to move the Qnifen column to the left of the Fiszol column:

1. In the Table Editor, move the cursor to cell D1, then press **Ctrl-F4** (Move), and select **3** (Column) and **1** (**M**ove). The Qnifen column disappears, and the message *Updating table* appears in the bottom-left corner of the screen.

2. With the cursor in cell C1, press **Enter** to retrieve the Qnifen column.

The Qnifen column reappears to the left of the Fiszol column:

```
┌─────────────────────────────────────────────────────────────────────┐
│║Percent Change│Adrenalin/Coca│Qnifen      ║Fiszol      ║             │
│║              │ine           │            ║            ║             │
│║Blood Pressure│250.6         │25.78       ║2.3         ║             │
│║Heart Rate    │5.78          │2.7         ║-3.67       ║             │
│║Brain         │12.0          │-34.28      ║2.466       ║             │
│║Stimulation   │              │            ║            ║             │
│║Bone Structure│0             │520.8       ║489.2       ║             │
│║Risk of Stroke│2.7           │1.56        ║0.91        ║             │
│                                                                       │
│                                                                       │
│ Table Edit:   Press Exit when done        Cell C1 Doc 1 Pg 3 Ln 1.14" Pos 4.35" │
│ ────────────────────────────────────────────────────────────────────│
│ Ctrl-Arrows Column Widths; Ins Insert; Del Delete; Move Move/Copy;    │
│ 1 Size; 2 Format; 3 Lines; 4 Header; 5 Math; 6 Options; 7 Join; 8 Split: 0 │
└─────────────────────────────────────────────────────────────────────┘
```

WordPerfect has renumbered the columns so that the Qnifen column is now column C and the Fiszol column is column D, but you are going to have to fix the line between the Qnifen and Fiszol columns manually, as follows:

1. With the cursor in cell C1, press **Alt-F4** (Block), and then press **Home,Down Arrow** to block the entire column.
2. Select **3** (**L**ines), **2** (**R**ight), and **2** (Single) to insert a single line between the columns.

Inserting rows   Suppose you want to use the *Percent Change* column heading as the table's title. The first step is to insert a new row at the top of the table. Follow these steps:

1. Press **Ctrl-Home** (Go To), type *a1*, and then press **Enter** to move the cursor to cell A1.
2. Press the **Ins** key, select **1** (**R**ows), and when the prompt *Number of Rows* appears, accept the default of 1 by pressing **Enter**.

WordPerfect displays the message *Updating table* and then returns the table to the screen with a new row of four columns inserted at the cursor. The cells have all been renumbered so that the first cell in the new row is now cell A1.

Joining cells   Next, we must join the cells of the new row to create one large cell, to accommodate the *Percent Change* heading. Joining cells is a simple two-step procedure.

Backing out of Table Editor menus	Inserting new columns	Deleting rows or columns
You can back out of any of the menus in the Table Editor by pressing F1 (Cancel). ♦	You can use the Ins key to insert a new column into a table. Simply follow the steps above for inserting a row, and when you get to step 2, select 2 (Columns) instead of 1 (Rows). Then specify the number of columns to be inserted, and press Enter. WordPerfect inserts the specified number of columns at the cursor. ♦	To delete rows or columns: 1. Move the cursor to the row or column you want to delete. 2. Press the Del key, select 1 (Rows) or 2 (Columns), and then enter the number of rows or columns to be deleted. You can restore rows and columns you have deleted by pressing F1 (Cancel). ♦

1. With the cursor located in cell A1 in the Table Editor, press **Alt-F4** (Block) and then press **End** to block cells A1 through D1.
2. Select **7** (**Join**), and when the prompt *Join cells?* appears, select **Y**(es).

The borders separating the columns in the first row disappear, creating one large cell. Now finish the task by moving the column heading:

Moving column headings

1. Press **F7** (Exit) to return to the Editing screen.
2. Move the cursor to cell A2, block *Percent Change*, press **Ctrl-F4** (Move), and select **1** (**Block**) and **1** (**Move**). The blocked text disappears.
3. Press **Shift-Tab** to move the cursor to cell A1, and then press **Enter** to retrieve *Percent Change* into that cell.
4. Move back to cell A2, and type *Drug* as the new column heading.

Here's the result:

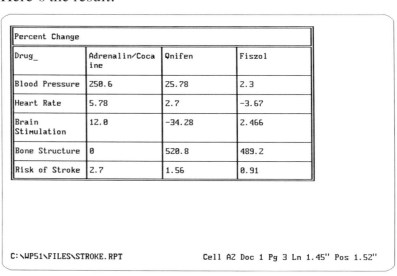

Percent Change			
Drug_	Adrenalin/Cocaine	Qnifen	Fiszol
Blood Pressure	250.6	25.78	2.3
Heart Rate	5.78	2.7	-3.67
Brain Stimulation	12.0	-34.28	2.466
Bone Structure	0	520.8	489.2
Risk of Stroke	2.7	1.56	0.91

C:\WP51\FILES\STROKE.RPT   Cell A2 Doc 1 Pg 3 Ln 1.45" Pos 1.52"

Changing row height and column width   You can adjust both row heights and column widths to suit your needs. You make these adjustments in the Table Editor.

You can set the row height to accommodate one line or multiple lines of text. With a single-line setting, text does not wrap within the cell and pressing Enter moves the cursor to the next cell. With a multi-line setting, text does wrap and pressing Enter moves the cursor to the next line within the cell. You can also select fixed or automatic row height. With a fixed setting, you enter the height for each row. With an automatic setting, WordPerfect adjusts the height based on the size of the text within the row.

You can set the column width by first selecting the Width option from the Column Format menu and then entering a specific measurement. You can also set the column width by holding down the Ctrl key and pressing the Left and Right Arrow keys.

Setting column widths

Let's change the heights of the rows and the widths of some of the columns in the example table:

1. Move the cursor to cell A1, press **Alt-F7** (Columns/ Table) to move to the Table Editor, and then block the entire table.
2. Select **2** (**F**ormat) and **3** (**R**ow Height), and then select **2** (Single Line: Au**t**o).

The rows in the table are reformatted, as you can see here:

```
┌─────────────────────────────────────────────────────────────────
│ Percent Change
│ ┌──────────────┬───────────────┬──────────┬──────────────┐
│ │Drug          │Adrenalin/Coca │Qnifen    │Fiszol        │
│ ├──────────────┼───────────────┼──────────┼──────────────┤
│ │Blood Pressure│250.6          │25.78     │2.3           │
│ ├──────────────┼───────────────┼──────────┼──────────────┤
│ │Heart Rate    │5.78           │2.7       │-3.67         │
│ ├──────────────┼───────────────┼──────────┼──────────────┤
│ │Brain         │12.0           │-34.28    │2.466         │
│ ├──────────────┼───────────────┼──────────┼──────────────┤
│ │Bone Structure│0              │520.8     │489.2         │
│ ├──────────────┼───────────────┼──────────┼──────────────┤
│ │Risk of Stroke│2.7            │1.56      │0.91          │
│ └──────────────┴───────────────┴──────────┴──────────────┘


│ Table Edit:  Press Exit when done       Cell A7 Doc 1 Pg 3 Ln 2.85" Pos 1.12"
│ ═══════════════════════════════════════════════════════════════════
│ Ctrl-Arrows Column Widths; Ins Insert; Del Delete; Move Move/Copy;
│ 1 Size; 2 Format; 3 Lines; 4 Header; 5 Math; 6 Options; 7 Join; 8 Split: 0
```

All the rows now contain single lines of text, some of which (such as *Stimulation* in cell A5) are not visible. WordPerfect won't print the hidden text, so we must adjust the column widths until all the text is visible. Follow these steps:

1. In the Table Editor, move the cursor to cell A2, and press **Ctrl-Right Arrow** until the entire word *Stimulation* is visible in cell A5.
2. Next, move the cursor to cell B2, and press **Ctrl-Right Arrow** until the entire word *Cocaine* is in view.

3. Move the cursor to cell C2, and press **Ctrl-Left Arrow** four times to decrease the width of column C. Repeat this procedure for column D.

All the text is now visible, as you can see here:

```
┌─────────────────────────────────────────────────────────────┐
│                                                              │
│ ┌───────────────────────────────────────────────────────┐   │
│ │Percent Change                                          │   │
│ ├────────────────┬─────────────────┬─────────┬──────────┤   │
│ │Drug            │Adrenalin/Cocaine│Qnifen   │Fiszol    │   │
│ ├────────────────┼─────────────────┼─────────┼──────────┤   │
│ │Blood Pressure  │250.6            │25.78    │2.3       │   │
│ ├────────────────┼─────────────────┼─────────┼──────────┤   │
│ │Heart Rate      │5.78             │2.7      │-3.67     │   │
│ ├────────────────┼─────────────────┼─────────┼──────────┤   │
│ │Brain Stimulation│12.0            │-34.28   │2.466     │   │
│ ├────────────────┼─────────────────┼─────────┼──────────┤   │
│ │Bone Structure  │0                │520.8    │489.2     │   │
│ ├────────────────┼─────────────────┼─────────┼──────────┤   │
│ │Risk of Stroke  │2.7              │1.56     │0.91      │   │
│ └────────────────┴─────────────────┴─────────┴──────────┘   │
│                                                              │
│                                                              │
│ Table Edit:  Press Exit when done      Cell D2 Doc 1 Pg 3 Ln 1.45" Pos 5.87" │
│ ─────────────────────────────────────────────────────────── │
│ Ctrl-Arrows Column Widths; Ins Insert; Del Delete; Move Move/Copy; │
│ 1 Size; 2 Format; 3 Lines; 4 Header; 5 Math; 6 Options; 7 Join; 8 Split: 0 │
└─────────────────────────────────────────────────────────────┘
```

Formatting tables   Having made all the necessary structural changes to the table, let's add some formatting. We'll format the title and headings and align the number entries on the decimal point. Here's how:

1. In the Table Editor, move the cursor to cell A1. To center *Percent Change*, the table title, select **2** (**Format**), **1** (**Cell**), **3** (**Justify**), and **2** (**Center**).

2. With the cursor still in cell A1, select **2** (**Format**), **1** (**Cell**), **2** (**Attributes**), **1** (**Size**), and **5** (**Large**) to make the title large. Then press **F6** (**Bold**) to make it bold.

3. Next, make the headings in the Drug column bold. Move the cursor to cell A2, and select **2** (**Format**), **2** (**Column**), **2** (**Attributes**), **2** (**Appearance**), and **1** (**Bold**).

4. To center-justify the headings in cells B2 through D2, move the cursor to cell B2, block the three headings, and follow step 1 above.

5. To decimal-align the numbers in the Adrenalin/Cocaine column, move the cursor to cell B3, and block cells B3 through B7. Then select **2** (**Format**), **1** (**Cell**), **3** (**Justify**), and **5** (**Decimal Align**).

6. Repeat the previous step to decimal-align the numbers in the Qnifen and Fiszol columns. (Be sure to place the

Decimal alignment

cursor in cells C3 and D3, respectively, before you block the cells in each column.)

That's it! Press **F7** (Exit) to return to the Editing screen, where the table looks like this:

Percent Change			
Drug	Adrenalin/Cocaine	Qnifen	Fiszol
Blood Pressure	250.6	25.78	2.3
Heart Rate	5.78	2.7	-3.67
Brain Stimulation	12.0	-34.28	2.46
Bone Structure	0	520.8	489.2
Risk of Stroke	2.7	1.56	0.91

C:\WP51\FILES\STROKE.RPT   Cell D7 Doc 1 Pg 3 Ln 2.88" Pos 6.48"

Changing gridlines   Before we wrap up this section, add a final touch to the table by changing the line below the title:

1. Press **Alt-F7** (Columns/Table) to move to the Table Editor, and move the cursor to cell A2.
2. Block cells A2 through D2. Select **3** (**L**ines), **3** (**T**op), and **2** (**S**ingle). A single line appears below cell A1.
3. Move the cursor to cell A1, and select **3** (**L**ines), **4** (**B**ottom), and **6** (**T**hick).

The result is this thick, shaded line below cell A1:

Percent Change			
Drug	Adrenalin/Cocaine	Qnifen	Fiszol
Blood Pressure	250.6	25.78	2.3
Heart Rate	5.78	2.7	-3.67
Brain Stimulation	12.0	-34.28	2.46
Bone Structure	0	520.8	489.2
Risk of Stroke	2.7	1.56	0.91

Table Edit: Press Exit when done   Cell A1 Doc 1 Pg 3 Ln 1.14" Pos 3.01"

Ctrl-Arrows Column Widths; Ins Insert; Del Delete; Move Move/Copy;
1 Size; 2 Format; 3 Lines; 4 Header; 5 Math; 6 Options; 7 Join; 8 Split; 0

Centering the table   With WordPerfect, you don't have to worry about adjusting margins to center the table on the page. A couple of selections do the trick:

1. In the Table Editor, select **6** (**O**ptions) to display the Table Options menu shown here:

```
Table Options

      1 - Spacing Between Text and Lines
            Left                            0.083"
            Right                           0.083"
            Top                             0.1"
            Bottom                          0"

      2 - Display Negative Results          1
              1 = with minus signs
              2 = with parentheses

      3 - Position of Table                 Left

      4 - Gray Shading (% of black)         10%








Selection: 0
```

2. Simply select **3** (**P**osition of Table), and then select **3** (**C**enter). Press **F7** (Exit) twice to return to the normal Editing screen.

When you print the report, the table will be centered between the left and right margins. For now, you can see how the Center option has affected the table by moving to the View Document screen). Then save the report without clearing the screen by pressing **F10** (Save).

Adding Page Headers

Take a look at pages two and three of the report shown at the beginning of the chapter. Both of the pages have a *header* at the top. A header is a line of text containing information, such as a report title, a date, or the name of your company, that you want to appear on the pages of your document. The advantage of using a header is that you create it once and then leave it up to WordPerfect to place it at the top of the pages for you. You can have two different headers on a page, and you can specify on which pages they should appear.

Follow these steps to create a header for the example report:

1. Press **Home,Home,Up Arrow** to move the cursor to the beginning of the report. (For the Header feature to work properly, the cursor must be at the top of the page on which you want the header to be printed.)
2. Press **Shift-F8** (Format), and select **2** (**P**age) from the Format menu. This Page Format menu appears:

```
Format: Page

    1 - Center Page (top to bottom)    No

    2 - Force Odd/Even Page

    3 - Headers

    4 - Footers

    5 - Margins - Top              1"
                Bottom             1"

    6 - Page Numbering

    7 - Paper Size                 8.5" x 11"
            Type                   Standard

    8 - Suppress (this page only)



Selection: 0
```

3. Select **3** (**H**eaders), **1** (Header **A**), and **2** (Every **P**age). WordPerfect displays the Header Editing screen, in which you enter the text of the header.
4. Type *Fox & Associates*. Then press **Alt-F6** (Flush Right), and type *Drug-Induced Stroke*.
5. Press **F7** (Exit) twice to save the header and return to the Editing screen.
6. To see the Header code [Header A:Every page;Fox & Associates[Flsh Rgt]Drug[-]Induced Stroke] at the beginning of the report, press **Alt-F3** (Reveal Codes). Press **Alt-F3** (Reveal Codes) again to return to the Editing screen.

Editing an Existing Header

You can change a header by displaying it in the Header Editing screen and editing it as you would in the normal Editing screen. When you move to the Header Editing screen, WordPerfect searches backward and then forward, displaying the first header it finds. To edit a specific header, place the cursor just after the desired Header code in the Reveal Codes screen before you move to the Header Editing screen.

For practice, edit the header you just created:

1. Press **Shift-F8** (Format), and select **2** (**P**age), **3** (**H**eaders), and **1** (Header **A**). Then select **5** (**E**dit). The Header Editing screen appears, displaying Header A.
2. To make the header small, block the entire header, press **Ctrl-F8** (Font), and select **1** (**S**ize) and **4** (**S**mall).
3. To make the header italic, reblock the header, press **Ctrl-F8** (Font), and select **2** (**A**ppearance) and **4** (**I**talc).
4. Press **F7** (Exit) twice to save the header and return to the Editing screen.

As with the footnote that you created earlier in the chapter, you cannot see the header in the Editing screen. You can, however, check it in the View Document screen by pressing **Shift-F7** (Print) and then selecting **6** (**V**iew Document). Press the **PgDn** key to see the header on the second and third pages. Then press **F7** (Exit) to return to the Editing screen, and save the report without clearing the screen by pressing **F10** (Save).

Suppressing Headers

You may have noticed in the View Document screen that the header on page one of the report is crowding the report title. To eliminate this problem, the first page of a document often does not have a header. Because headers often contain the

---

Headers that stand out

Adding attributes to the header, such as small type and italic, will help it stand out from the rest of the text in the document. ♦

Multiple headers

You can create two different headers for each page of your document by designating one as Header A and the other as Header B. You can place both of the headers on the same page, or you can place one header on even-numbered pages and one on odd-numbered pages. ♦

Footers

You can create footers, which appear at the bottom of the page, by using the procedures described for headers, except that you'll want to select 4 (Footers) from the Page Format menu instead of 3 (Headers). ♦

same information as the document's title page, suppressing
the header on this page also avoids redundancy.

Follow these steps to suppress Header A on page one of
the example report:

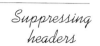

*Suppressing
headers*

1. Press **Home,Home,Up Arrow** to move the cursor to
   the beginning of the report. (The Suppress feature
   affects only the page on which the cursor is currently
   located.)
2. Press **Shift-F8** (Format), select **2** (**P**age), and then
   select **8** (**S**uppress). The Format: Suppress menu appears, as shown below:

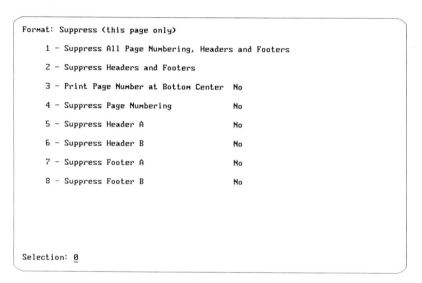

```
Format: Suppress (this page only)

     1 - Suppress All Page Numbering, Headers and Footers

     2 - Suppress Headers and Footers

     3 - Print Page Number at Bottom Center  No

     4 - Suppress Page Numbering             No

     5 - Suppress Header A                    No

     6 - Suppress Header B                    No

     7 - Suppress Footer A                    No

     8 - Suppress Footer B                    No




Selection: 0
```

3. Select **5** (Suppress **H**eader A), and then select **Y**(es) to
   suppress Header A on the first page.
4. Press **F7** (Exit) to return to the Editing screen.

You can see the Suppress code [Suppress:HA] at the beginning of the report in the Reveal Codes screen, and you can
see that the first-page header has been suppressed in the View
Document screen. Back at the Editing screen, save the report
by pressing **F10** (Save).

Numbering Pages

WordPerfect's Page Numbering feature is easy to use and
efficient. You can print numbers in one of eight different
positions on the page and in one of three different numbering

schemes—Arabic (1, 2, 3), lowercase Roman (i, ii, iii), or uppercase Roman (I, II, III).

Follow these steps to number the pages of the report:

1. Press **Home,Home,Up Arrow** to move the cursor to the top of the report. (For page numbering to work correctly, the cursor must be located at the beginning of the page where you want numbering to begin.)

2. Press **Shift-F8** (Format), select **2** (**P**age), and select **6** (Page **N**umbering) from the Page Format menu. This Format: Page Numbering menu appears:

```
Format: Page Numbering

    1 - New Page Number        1

    2 - Page Number Style      ^B

    3 - Insert Page Number

    4 - Page Number Position No page numbering




Selection: 0
```

Suppressing page numbers

You can also use the Suppress feature to keep page numbers from being printed on selected pages. (Suppressing page numbers does not disrupt the page numbering in your document.) ♦

Customizing pages numbers

You can use the Page Number Style option on the Format: Page Numbering menu to insert text along with the page number. You can type up to 30 characters, including characters from the WordPerfect character sets (see page 99). For example, to insert the word *Page* before every page number, select 2 (Page Number Style),

and type the word *Page* followed by a space. The page-number style must include a ^B code, which represents the actual page number. If you forget to include the code by pressing Ctrl-B, WordPerfect will insert it for you. ♦

3. Accept the default setting of 1 for the New Page Number option.

4. Select **4** (Page Number **P**osition) to display the eight possible numbering positions:

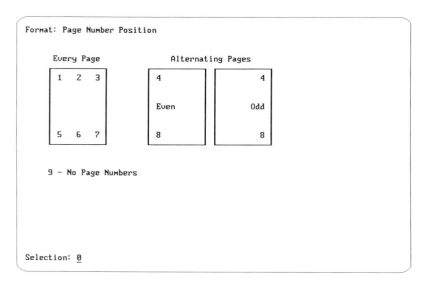

```
Format: Page Number Position


    Every Page                    Alternating Pages
    ┌─────────────┐        ┌─────────────┐ ┌─────────────┐
    │  1   2   3  │        │ 4           │ │           4 │
    │             │        │             │ │             │
    │             │        │  Even       │ │       Odd   │
    │             │        │             │ │             │
    │  5   6   7  │        │ 8           │ │           8 │
    └─────────────┘        └─────────────┘ └─────────────┘

       9 - No Page Numbers




    Selection: 0
```

5. Select **6** (Bottom Center) to print a page number at the bottom center of every page, and press **F7** (Exit) to return to the Editing screen.

When you selected the Page Numbering feature, WordPerfect inserted the Page Numbering code [Pg Numbering:Bottom Center]. You can see this code at the beginning of the report in the Reveal Codes screen.

From Arabic to Roman

To change the page numbering scheme in a document from Arabic to lowercase or uppercase Roman, type *i* (for lowercase Roman) or *I* (for uppercase Roman) at the New Page Number option on the Format : Page Numbering menu (see step 3 above). ♦

Line numbering

You can use WordPerfect's Line Numbering feature on the Line Format menu to place a number adjacent to every line of text in a document. (Footnotes and endnotes are included in line numbering; headers and footers are not.) Line numbers are useful in documents such as legal contracts, where particular lines might need to be referenced.

To turn on line numbering: **1.** Be sure the cursor is at the location where you want line numbering to begin. **2.** Press Shift-F8 (Format), and select 1 (Line). **3.** Select 5 (Line Numbering) and Y(es). **4.** When the Format: Line Numbering menu appears, select the desired options, and then press F7 (Exit) to return to the Editing screen. ♦

Viewing page numbers

In the View Document screen, you can see the page numbers, which do not appear in the Editing screen. Press **Shift-F7** (Print), and select **6** (View Document) and **3** (Full Page) to see the number on the first page. Select **4** (Facing Pages), and then press the **PgDn** key to see the numbers on the second and third pages. To get a closer look, select **1** (100%) and **Home,Down Arrow**.

Back at the Editing screen, save the report without clearing the screen by pressing **F10** (Save).

Selecting a Base Font and Printing the Report

At last you're ready to select a base font and print the report. You can select fonts for some features, such as footnotes and headers, in the special editing screens that appear when those features are selected. But unless you need fancy formatting for these elements, it's quicker to select a base font for the entire document by changing the Initial Base Font setting in the Document Format menu. Changing the settings in the Document Format menu is similar to changing the settings of the Initial Codes option on the Setup: Initial Settings menu (see page 61), except that the base font selected in Document Format affects only the current document, not all subsequent WordPerfect documents.

Setting document defaults

You can enter codes as defaults in the Initial Codes option on the Document Format menu just as you would in the Initial Codes option on the Setup: Initial Settings menu (see Chapter 3). Some examples of codes that can be entered are justification, margins, and line spacing. ♦

Overriding defaults

Keep in mind that settings in the Document Format menu affect only the current document, overriding any settings made in the Initial Codes option on the Setup: Initial Settings menu. And any settings you make in the document itself override the base-font settings in the Document Format menu, so you can change the font of individual elements. For example, you might want to change the font of the report title to give it a little more distinction (we used Swiss for the title of our report). ♦

Here's how to select a base font for the report:

1. Press **Home,Home,Up Arrow** to move the cursor to the beginning of the document.

2. Press **Shift-F8** (Format), and select **3** (Document) and **3** (Initial Base Font). The Base Font menu appears.

3. Move the highlight to the desired font (such as Dutch Roman 12pt), and press **Enter**. You then return to the Document Format menu where the name of the font you selected appears in the Initial Base Font option.

4. Press **F7** (Exit) to return to the Editing screen.

5. Press **Home,Down Arrow** to reformat the document.

With your font(s) selected, you're ready to print the report. You can select 1 (Full Document) to print the entire document, 2 (Page) to print only the page on which the cursor is currently located, and 5 (Multiple Pages) to print more than one page. (To print the second and third pages, enter *2-3*; to print the first and third pages, enter *1,3*.)

Finally, save the report one more time, so that you can use it in the next chapter where we discuss ways of dressing up documents with information created in other programs.

6

Graphic Impact

Ready-made graphics
Page 126

Creating a logo
Page 128

DRUG-INDUCED STROKE

Risk Factors

A number of important health conditions are now recognized as contributing to the cause of stroke in humans. These include:

Age: The incidence of stroke increases dramatically with age. The chances of stroke are very small in young individuals. A sharp increase in the risk of stroke occurs in the population beyond 50 years of age.

Hypertension: The risk of stroke incre— s that of heart disease in humans who have elevated blood pressure. It has now — by clinical trials that control of blood pressure is a major factor in redu— . Furthermore, the sooner increased blood pressure is diagnosed — ion of stroke as well as heart attack.

Smoking — e. The longer an individual has smoked — troke as well as heart attack. It is — he duration of smoking will — Whether the same is true for — 'll apply.

Fox & Associates   *Drug-Induced Stroke*

produce damage to blood vessels which weaken their walls and, in the case of arteries in the brain, may lead to stroke. The evidence for the way in which these drugs produce this effect is not clear, but it is thought that it occurs in — owing steps:

1. With continual administrati— of time, the drug accumulates in the cells th—

2. As the drug accumulat— processes.

3. Eventually, the cells — and vulnerable.

Qnifen and Fiszol: B— bone). Both have also been— drugs is given below:

Qnifen was the — for use in os— after several y— associated w—

Although both— differ greatly— has none.— incidence — in the Ne—

Wrapping text around graphics
Page 131

Fox & Associates   *Drug-Induced Stroke*

Percent Change			
Drug	Adrenalin/Cocaine	Qnifen	Fiszol
Blood Pressure	250.6	25.78	2.3
Heart Rate	5.78	2.7	-3.67
Brain Stimulation	12.0	-34.28	2.46
Bone Structure	0	520.8	489.2
Risk of Stroke	2.7	1.56	0.91

The data displayed in the figure were obtained from a clinical study of 560 adult patients with normal blood pressures. The subjects were treated with the Qnifen doses indicated for a period of three weeks. Their blood pressures were recorded at that time and plotted against dose.

Converting graphics to .WPG format
Page 130

PATIENT	SEX	WEIGHT	BP	PULSE
G.W.	M	178	152	80
S.H.	F	124	120	63
B.P.	F	132	145	79
P.J.	M	198	134	70
D.E.	M	205	168	90

Importing a range
Page 134

3

S uccessful computer applications have to be "friendly" toward their users, and in previous chapters, you have seen how easy WordPerfect is to learn and use. But these days, user-friendliness is not enough. Any application that aspires to best-seller status must also be friendly toward other applications. In this chapter, we'll show you how easily you can incorporate files that you've created in other applications into your WordPerfect documents, by using WordPerfect's Graphics Conversion Program and Graphics feature. Depending on your printer's capabilities, you may be able to dress up your documents with charts, spreadsheet information, and many different kinds of graphics.

Importing WordPerfect's Graphics

In Chapter 4, you merged letterheads with the letter you created in Chapter 3. The letterheads were separate text files that, after the merge, became part of the letter file. In a similar way, you can merge separate graphics files into your Word-Perfect documents.

Ready-made graphics

The WordPerfect 5.1 software package includes a number of ready-made graphics files that are suitable for many different types of documents. We'll use one of these files (SCALE.WPG) to demonstrate how easy it is to import graphics with WordPerfect. To follow along, the graphics files, which have .WPG extensions, must be stored in the main WordPerfect directory, WP51, on your hard disk. (You probably copied the graphics files when you installed the program. If you didn't, you should copy them now.) Then, with WordPerfect loaded and the report document displayed on your screen, follow these steps:

1. Press **Home,Home,Up Arrow** to move to the top of the report.
2. Press **Alt-F9** (Graphics), select **1** (Figure) and **1** (Create). This Definition: Figure menu appears:

```
Definition: Figure

    1 - Filename

    2 - Contents          Empty

    3 - Caption

    4 - Anchor Type       Paragraph

    5 - Vertical Position  0"

    6 - Horizontal Position  Right

    7 - Size              3.25" wide x 3.25" (high)

    8 - Wrap Text Around Box Yes

    9 - Edit




Selection: 0
```

3. Select **1** (**F**ilename), type *scale.wpg*, and press **Enter**.
   The setting in the Contents option changes from Empty
   to Graphic.
4. Press **F7** (Exit) to return to the Editing screen.

You cannot see the graphic itself in the Editing screen. All
you see is a box labeled *FIG 1* on the right side of the screen,
as shown here:

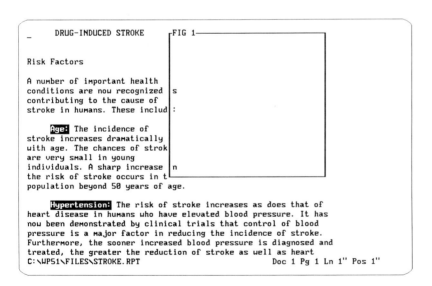

If any text spills over into the graphics box, it's probably
because you're using a proportionally spaced font. Everything will be fine when the report is printed. Now, move

to the Reveal Codes screen to see the Figure Box code [Fig Box:1;SCALE.WPG;] that WordPerfect has inserted. Then move to the View Document screen to see the graphic, which looks like this:

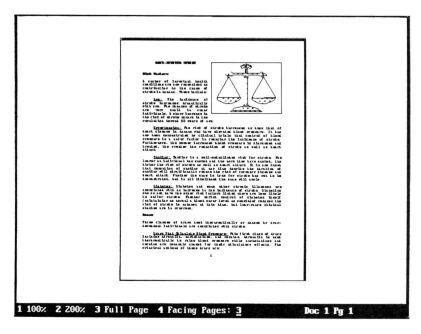

(If your computer does not have a graphics card, Word-Perfect can display only a rough approximation of the image.)

Changing the Graphic's Size

After you import the graphic, you can change its size and shape to suit the needs of your document. Let's turn the graphic into a small logo. Here's how:

Creating a logo

1. Press **Alt-F9** (Graphics), and select **1** (**F**igure) and **2** (**E**dit).
2. When the *Figure number?* prompt appears, type *1* for Figure 1, and press **Enter**.
3. To left-justify the graphic, select **6** (**H**orizontal Position) and **1** (**L**eft).
4. To change the width of the graphics box, select **7** (**S**ize) and **1** (Set **W**idth/Auto Height). With this option, Word-Perfect automatically adjusts the height of the graphics box as you change the width, to maintain the original scale of the image.
5. When the *Width =* prompt appears, type *1* (for 1 inch), and then press **Enter**.

Now use the Graphics Editor to make some more changes:

1. Select **9** (**E**dit) from the Definition: Figure menu. This Graphics Editor screen appears, displaying the image of the scale from the SCALE.WPG file and, at the bottom of the screen, several editing keys and an editing options menu:

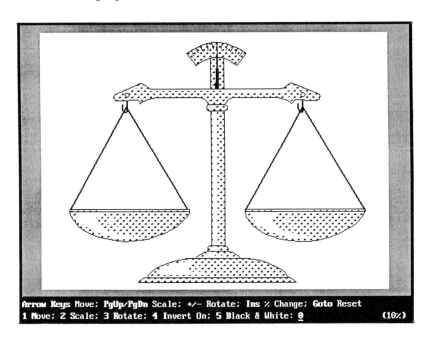

2. To decrease the size of the scale, press **PgDn** twice.
3. Press the **Down Arrow** key once to move the scale toward the bottom of the graphics box.

Rotating and flipping graphics

You can rotate and flip a graphic in the Graphics Editor, like this: **1.** Select 3 (Rotate) from the menu at the bottom of the Graphics Editor. **2.** Type *180*, and press Enter to rotate the scale 180 degrees. **3.** When the *Mirror image?* prompt appears, select Y(es) to flip, or create a mirror image, of the graphic. ♦

Clockwise or counterclockwise

While in the Graphics Editor, you can rotate graphics clockwise or counterclockwise by pressing + (numeric keypad) or − (numeric keypad), respectively. The image is rotated the percentage displayed in the bottom-right corner of the screen. ♦

Restoring original size and orientation

If you want to return a graphics image in the Graphics Editor to its original size and orientation, simply press Ctrl-Home (Go To). ♦

Now return to the Editing screen by pressing **F7** (Exit) twice. From there, go to the View Document screen to see the changes you made to the graphic, which should now be small and left-justified. If your printer can handle graphics, print the first page of the report and take a look at the new logo. Then save the report and exit WordPerfect by pressing **F7** (Exit).

Importing Graphics Created with Other Applications

Converting graphics to .WPG format

WordPerfect can use only graphics files that have been converted to a format called *.WPG*. The conversion work is handled by the Graphics Conversion Program, which accepts files in a variety of graphics formats and converts them to .WPG format. To be able to use the Graphics Conversion Program, you must first be sure that the graphic you want to import has been saved in one of the supported formats—EPS, PCX, and TIFF are some common examples.

In this section, we will demonstrate how to convert a graphics file in a supported format to the .WPG format. Then we'll import the graphic into the report. If you have a graphic available, you can follow along. We'll use this graphics file:

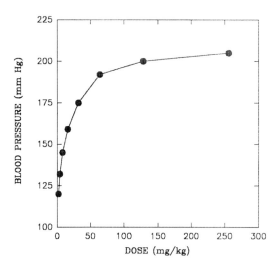

This chart, which is stored in a file called QNIFEN.PLT, was created with the SigmaPlot program. (If you want to follow along, you can use your own graphics file.) Because the

SigmaPlot format is not supported by WordPerfect, we saved QNIFEN.PLT while in SigmaPlot in the HPGL (Hewlett-Packard Graphics Language) format, which is supported. Then we used WordPerfect's Graphics Conversion Program to convert the HPGL format to the .WPG format, like this:

1. Be sure you're at the C> prompt. Then change to the directory where the Graphics Conversion Program (GRAPHCNV.EXE) is stored, by typing *cd c:\wp51* and pressing **Enter**.

2. To start the conversion program, type *graphcnv*, and press **Enter**.

3. Type the full pathname of the file you want to convert (in this case, we'll type *c:\wp51\files\qnifen.plt*), and press **Enter**.

4. Type the full pathname of the converted file (in this case, *c:\wp51\files\qnifen.wpg*), and press **Enter**.

5. The conversion program displays a *Converting* message. Then, after the file is converted, you see the message —> *ok* and the prompt *Press any key to continue*. Press any key to exit the conversion program.

We can now import the QNIFEN.WPG file into the report. The steps are simple:

1. With WordPerfect loaded and the report document on the screen, move the cursor to the desired location (in this case, a couple of lines below the table at the end of the report).

2. Press **Alt-F9** (Graphics), and select **1** (**Figure**) and **1** (**Create**).

3. From the Definition: Figure menu, select **1** (**Filename**), type *qnifen.wpg*, and press **Enter**.

4. Press **F7** (Exit) to return to the Editing screen.

Next, move to the View Documents screen to see whether any adjustments are needed. For this example, we returned to the Editing screen and then to the Definition: Figure menu (Alt-F9,1,2,2), selected the Size option, and decreased the width and height of the graphics box. Back at the Editing screen, we added some text to the report. Because the Wrap Text Around Box option in the Definition: Figure menu was

Wrapping text around graphics

set to the default Y(es), the text we added wrapped around the graphics box. Then, with the cursor on the Figure Box code in the Reveal Codes screen, we removed the border surrounding the graphic by selecting the Border Style option from the Graphics Options menu (Alt-F9,1,4,1) and selecting None for the Left, Right, Top, and Bottom borders. Finally, we printed the last page of the report, and this is the result:

Fox & Associates   *Drug-Induced Stroke*

Percent Change			
Drug	Adrenalin/Cocaine	Qnifen	Fiszol
Blood Pressure	250.6	25.78	2.3
Heart Rate	5.78	2.7	-3.67
Brain Stimulation	12.0	-34.28	2.46
Bone Structure	0	520.8	489.2
Risk of Stroke	2.7	1.56	0.91

The data displayed in the figure were obtained from a clinical study of 560 adult patients with normal blood pressures. The subjects were treated with the Qnifen doses indicated for a period of three weeks. Their blood pressures were recorded at that time and plotted against dose.

Importing Spreadsheets

Although WordPerfect's Table feature allows you to create impressive tables and do some mathematics with ease, it doesn't calculate complex formulas and functions the way a spreadsheet program does. And although a spreadsheet program is great for performing calculations, it lacks the word-processing capabilities you need to put together dynamic reports. Suppose you have gone to a lot of trouble to create a spreadsheet of data and you now want to include that data in a report. It would be frustrating to have to rekey all that information into a WordPerfect table for presentation. Fortunately, you don't have to. By using WordPerfect's Spreadsheet Import feature, you can combine the best of both worlds—the numeric know-how of a spreadsheet program with the word-processing proficiency of WordPerfect.

To demonstrate, we'll pull this spreadsheet, which was created with Lotus 1-2-3, into the report:

```
A1: (G) 'PATIENT                                                      READY


        A       B        C       D        E       F        G        H
 1   PATIENT  SEX     WEIGHT    BP      PULSE    EEG     BONE/DEN
 2   G.W.     M          178   152        80       4      23.5
 3   S.H.     F          124   120        63       8      16.3
 4   B.P.     F          132   145        79       9      12.7
 5   P.J.     M          198   134        70       8      31.7
 6   D.E.     M          205   168        90       7      30.9
 7   C.E.     M          212   136        72       5      24.9
 8   W.D.     F          156   127        65       5      17.9
 9   T.W.     F          127   140        85       3      14.8
10   L.D.     F          117   128        69       7      20.7
11   G.A.     F          167   137        85       8      10.7
12   J.K.     M          179   148        74       5      22.7
13   A.M.     M          158   143        81       4      32.9
14
15
16
17
18
19
20
25-Mar-91  05:50 PM       UNDO
```

You can follow these steps with your own spreadsheet file:

1. Insert blank lines to move the cursor below the chart at the end of the report. Then press **Ctrl-F5** (Text In/Out), and select **5** (**S**preadsheet) and **1** (**I**mport). This menu appears:

```
Spreadsheet: Import

    1 - Filename

    2 - Range

    3 - Type              Table

    4 - Perform Import













    Selection: 0
```

Importing a range

2. Select **1** (**F**ilename), type the full path and filename of the spreadsheet to be imported (in this case, we typed *c:\wp51\files\qnifen.wk1*), and press **Enter**.

3. If you don't want to import the entire spreadsheet, select **2** (**R**ange), type the range of cells that you want to import, separating the first cell from the last cell in the range by a colon, one period, or two periods (for example A1..E6), and press **Enter**.

4. To import the spreadsheet file as a WordPerfect table, accept the default setting of Table for the Type option, and then select **4** (**P**erform Import).

WordPerfect displays the message * *Importing Spreadsheet* * and returns you to the Editing screen, where the spreadsheet file has been imported as a table at the cursor.

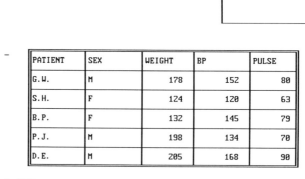

PATIENT	SEX	WEIGHT	BP	PULSE
G.W.	M	178	152	80
S.H.	F	124	120	63
B.P.	F	132	145	79
P.J.	M	198	134	70
D.E.	M	205	168	90

C:\WP51\FILES\STROKE.RPT   Doc 1 Pg 4 Ln 6.26" Pos 1"

Choosing files from the List Files screen

If you can't remember the name of the spreadsheet file you need, after you select 1 (Filename) you can press F5 (List), and enter the path of the directory where the spreadsheet file is located. Then press Enter to display the files in that directory, highlight the desired file, and select 1 (Retrieve) to retrieve the file for importing. ♦

Supported spreadsheet formats

Currently, files from the spreadsheet programs listed below can be imported into WordPerfect documents:

PlanPerfect

Lotus 1-2-3 (up to Release 3.0)

Excel 2.x

Symphony

Quattro and Quattro Pro ♦

Linking spreadsheets

When you're ready to use the more advanced Spreadsheet Link feature to establish links between spreadsheets and WordPerfect documents, turn to the sections entitled "Spreadsheet, Import and Link" and "Spreadsheet, Link Options" in the *WordPerfect Reference Manual.* ♦

You can then edit the table, both in the Editing screen and in the Table Editor. Here is the last page of the report, showing the demonstration spreadsheet data:

Fox & Associates   *Drug-Induced Stroke*

Percent Change			
Drug	Adrenalin/Cocaine	Qnifen	Fiszol
Blood Pressure	250.6	25.78	2.3
Heart Rate	5.78	2.7	-3.67
Brain Stimulation	12.0	-34.28	2.46
Bone Structure	0	520.8	489.2
Risk of Stroke	2.7	1.56	0.91

The data displayed in the figure were obtained from a clinical study of 560 adult patients with normal blood pressures. The subjects were treated with the Qnifen doses indicated for a period of three weeks. Their blood pressures were recorded at that time and plotted against dose.

PATIENT	SEX	WEIGHT	BP	PULSE
G.W.	M	178	152	80
S.H.	F	124	120	63
B.P.	F	132	145	79
P.J.	M	198	134	70
D.E.	M	205	168	90

3

By itself, WordPerfect can create some pretty snazzy documents. Add a few graphics and a spreadsheet, and you've got documents with real distinction! WordPerfect's Graphics and Spreadsheet Import features allow you to tap into valuable outside resources. So be adventurous, and let WordPerfect help you generate a report that will make your colleagues sit up and take notice.

7

Time-Saving Form Documents

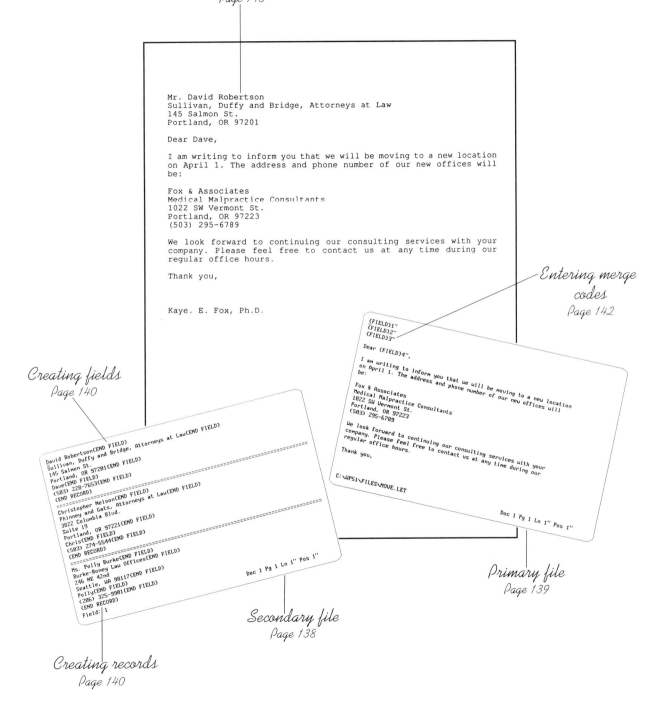

Printing the merged file
Page 143

Mr. David Robertson
Sullivan, Duffy and Bridge, Attorneys at Law
145 Salmon St.
Portland, OR 97201

Dear Dave,

I am writing to inform you that we will be moving to a new location
on April 1. The address and phone number of our new offices will
be:

Fox & Associates
Medical Malpractice Consultants
1022 SW Vermont St.
Portland, OR 97223
(503) 295-6789

We look forward to continuing our consulting services with your
company. Please feel free to contact us at any time during our
regular office hours.

Thank you,

Kaye. E. Fox, Ph.D.

Entering merge codes
Page 142

{FIELD}1~
{FIELD}2~
{FIELD}3~

Dear {FIELD}4~,

I am writing to inform you that we will be moving to a new location
on April 1. The address and phone number of our new offices will
be:

Fox & Associates
Medical Malpractice Consultants
1022 SW Vermont St.
Portland, OR 97223
(503) 295-6789

We look forward to continuing our consulting services with your
company. Please feel free to contact us at any time during our
regular office hours.

Thank you,

C:\WP51\FILES\MOVE.LET

Doc 1 Pg 1 Ln 1" Pos 1"

Primary file
Page 139

Creating fields
Page 140

David Robertson{END FIELD}
Sullivan, Duffy and Bridge, Attorneys at Law{END FIELD}
145 Salmon St.
Portland, OR 97201{END FIELD}
Dave{END FIELD}
(503) 228-7653{END FIELD}
{END RECORD}
==================================
Christopher Nelson{END FIELD}
Phinney and Gats, Attorneys at Law{END FIELD}
3822 Columbia Blvd.
Suite 19
Portland, OR 97221{END FIELD}
Chris{END FIELD}
(503) 274-5544{END FIELD}
{END RECORD}
==================================
Ms. Polly Burke{END FIELD}
Burke-Roney Law Offices{END FIELD}
246 NE 42nd
Seattle, WA 98117{END FIELD}
Polly{END FIELD}
(206) 325-9981{END FIELD}
{END RECORD}
Field: 1

Doc 1 Pg 1 Ln 1" Pos 1"

Secondary file
Page 138

Creating records
Page 140

If you need to send the same letter to half a dozen of your clients, you can create a template letter and quickly fill in the name, address, and salutation for each client. But what if you need to send the letter to a hundred clients? And what if you communicate regularly with the same set of clients? Isn't there a way to save having to type those names and addresses over and over again?

The time-saver you're looking for is WordPerfect's Merge feature. You can use Merge to create "personalized" letters and envelopes for mass mailings, as well as a whole host of other documents, such as phone lists, invoices, memos, and contracts. To use the Merge feature properly, you need to be familiar with some jargon, so we'll start with a few definitions, using a form letter as an example. To create a form letter, you need to create a *primary file* and a *secondary file*. Let's talk about the secondary file first.

Secondary file →

The *secondary file* contains the information that changes from letter to letter, such as the names and addresses of the recipients. Collectively, the information that will be merged into one letter—in this case, a name, company name, address, and salutation—is referred to as a *record*, and each item within one record is referred to as a *field*. To understand this relationship, take a look at this secondary file:

```
David Robertson{END FIELD}
Sullivan, Duffy and Bridge, Attorneys at Law{END FIELD}
145 Salmon St.
Portland, OR 97201{END FIELD}
Dave{END FIELD}
(503) 228-7653{END FIELD}
{END RECORD}
================================================================================
Christopher Nelson{END FIELD}
Phinney and Gats, Attorneys at Law{END FIELD}
3822 Columbia Blvd.
Suite 19
Portland, OR 97221{END FIELD}
Chris{END FIELD}
(503) 274-5544{END FIELD}
{END RECORD}
================================================================================
Ms. Polly Burke{END FIELD}
Burke-Roney Law Offices{END FIELD}
246 NE 42nd
Seattle, WA 98117{END FIELD}
Polly{END FIELD}
(206) 325-9901{END FIELD}
{END RECORD}
Field: 1                                                 Doc 1 Pg 1 Ln 1" Pos 1"
```

The records are separated by {END RECORD} codes, followed by hard page breaks. The fields within each record are separated by {END FIELD} codes followed by hard returns.

You can include as many records as you want (or as many as disk space permits) in a secondary file, and you can include an unlimited number of fields in each record. However, every record must contain the same number of fields, and every field must either contain the same type of information or be empty. For example, field 5 of every record in the example contains a phone number. If you have a record with no phone number, field 5 of that record remains empty but still ends with an {END FIELD} code and a hard return.

The *primary file* contains the information that does not change from letter to letter—the text of the letter. This file also controls the merging process by means of codes that you insert as placeholders for the information that does change from letter to letter. Here's an example:

Primary file

```
{FIELD}1~
{FIELD}2~
{FIELD}3~

Dear {FIELD}4~,

I am writing to inform you that we will be moving to a new location
on April 1. The address and phone number of our new offices will
be:

Fox & Associates
Medical Malpractice Consultants
1022 SW Vermont St.
Portland, OR 97223
(503) 295-6789

We look forward to continuing our consulting services with your
company. Please feel free to contact us at any time during our
regular office hours.

Thank you,


C:\WP51\FILES\MOVE.LET                       Doc 1 Pg 1 Ln 1" Pos 1"
```

The {FIELD}1~ merge code is a placeholder for the information contained in field 1 in the records of the secondary file. The tilde (~) tells WordPerfect that the number 1 is part of the code and not part of the text of the letter.

Creating a Form Letter

Let's create the example primary and secondary files so that you can see how merging works. Because you will probably use the same secondary file with more than one primary file, you'll usually start by creating the secondary file, which in this case is a "database" of clients' names and addresses.

Creating the Secondary File

Each record in the secondary file we're going to create contains five fields: names in field 1, company names in field 2, addresses in field 3, salutation names in field 4, and phone numbers in field 5. Fields do not have to contain the same number of characters or even the same number of lines. For example, field 3 in the second record might contain an address that is three lines long, whereas field 3 in the third record might contain an address that is only two lines long.

Load WordPerfect, and starting with a clear screen, follow these steps to create the secondary file, using the suggested names and addresses or some of your own:

Creating fields →

1. In a clear Editing screen, type *David Robertson*, and press **F9** (End Field) to insert an {END FIELD} code and a hard return at the end of the line. You've just created your first field.
2. On the second line, type *Sullivan, Duffy and Bridge, Attorneys at Law*, and press **F9** (End Field) to insert an {END FIELD} code and a hard return.
3. On the third and fourth lines, type the following, and press **F9** (End Field) after the Zip Code:

   145 Salmon St.
   Portland, OR 97201

4. On the fifth line, type *Dave*, and press **F9** (End Field).
5. On the sixth line, type *(503) 228-7653*, and press **F9** (End Field).

Creating records →

6. To end the record, press **Shift-F9** (Merge Codes), and select **2** (**E**nd Record). WordPerfect inserts an {END RECORD} code and a hard page break at the cursor. Here's what your first record looks like:

```
David Robertson{END FIELD}
Sullivan, Duffy and Bridge, Attorneys at Law{END FIELD}
145 Salmon St.
Portland, OR 97201{END FIELD}
Dave{END FIELD}
(503) 228-7653{END FIELD}
{END RECORD}
=============================================================================
-
```

Now you can enter a couple of other records. Follow the preceding steps to enter the following information. Press **F9** after each field, and press **Shift-F9** (Merge Codes) and select **2** (**E**nd Record) after each record.

> *Christopher Nelson*
> *Phinney and Gats, Attorneys at Law*
> *3822 Columbia Blvd.*
> *Suite 19*
> *Portland, OR 97221*
> *Chris*
> *(503) 274-5544*
>
> *Ms. Polly Burke*
> *Burke-Roney Law Offices*
> *246 NE 42nd*
> *Seattle, WA 98117*
> *Polly*
> *(206) 325-9901*

The secondary file now looks like the one on page 138. Press **F7** (Exit) to save the file with the name *clients*, and then clear the screen.

Creating the Primary File

Now we're ready to create a primary file that makes use of the secondary file's name and address database. Be sure the Editing screen is clear, and then follow these steps:

1. Press **Enter** twice, and type the following:

   I am writing to inform you that we will be moving to a new location on April 1. The address and phone number of our new offices will be:

   Fox & Associates
   Medical Malpractice Consultants
   1022 SW Vermont St.
   Portland, OR 97223
   (503) 295-6789

We look forward to continuing our consulting services with your company. Please feel free to contact us at any time during our regular office hours.

Thank you,

Kaye E. Fox, Ph.D.

2. Press **Home,Home,Up Arrow** to move the cursor to the beginning of the letter, where you are going to insert the first placeholder merge code.

3. Press **Shift-F9** (Merge Codes), and select **1** (Field). Type *1* at the *Enter Field* prompt, and press **Enter**. WordPerfect inserts a {FIELD}1˜ merge code.

Entering merge codes

4. Press **Enter** to start a new line, press **Shift-F9** (Merge Codes), and select **1** (Field). Type *2*, and press **Enter** to insert a {FIELD}2˜ merge code.

5. Repeat the previous step, typing *3* at the *Enter Field* prompt to insert a {FIELD}3˜ merge code.

6. Press **Enter** twice below the {FIELD}3˜ merge code, and then type *Dear* followed by a space.

7. Without moving the cursor, press **Shift-F9** (Merge Codes), select **1** (Field), type *4*, and press **Enter** to insert a {FIELD}4˜ merge code after the word *Dear*.

8. Finally, type a comma after the {FIELD}4˜ code.

Your primary file now looks like the one on page 139. Press **F7** (Exit) to save the primary file with the name *move.let*, and then clear the screen.

Merging and Printing the Files

This is the moment of truth. If you have inserted the codes correctly, merging the primary and secondary files will be a piece of cake. Just follow these steps:

1. With a clear screen, press **Ctrl-F9** (Merge/Sort), and select **1** (**Merge**).

2. When the *Primary file* prompt appears, type *move.let*, and press **Enter**.

3. When the *Secondary file* prompt appears, type *clients*, and press **Enter**.

As WordPerfect merges the two files, it displays the message * *Merging* *. When the merging process is complete, you are returned to the Editing screen. You can then view and print the merged letters. Here's how:

1. Press **Home,Home,Up Arrow** to move the cursor to the top of the first letter, which looks like this:

```
David Robertson
Sullivan, Duffy and Bridge, Attorneys at Law
145 Salmon St.
Portland, OR 97201

Dear Dave,

I am writing to inform you that we will be moving to a new location
on April 1. The address and phone number of our new offices will
be:

Fox & Associates
Medical Malpractice Consultants
1822 SW Vermont St.
Portland, OR 97223
(503) 295-6789

We look forward to continuing our consulting services with your
company. Please feel free to contact us at any time during our
regular office hours.

Thank you,


                                     Doc 1 Pg 1 Ln 1" Pos 1"
```

2. Press the **PgDn** key to move to the top of the second letter, and then press **PgDn** to move to the third letter. As you can see, WordPerfect replaced the merge codes in the primary file with the names and addresses from the secondary file to create a "personalized" letter for each record.
3. Press **F10** (Save), and save the document containing the letters as *move.mrg*.
4. Press **Shift-F7** (Print), and select **1** (Full Document) to print the letters. Because the letters are separated by hard page breaks, they print on separate pages.

Printing the merged file

Press **F7** (Exit) to exit MOVE.MRG and clear the screen.

Editing the Primary File

You can use a field more than once in a primary file. For example, you can delete the words *your firm* from the second paragraph of MOVE.LET and insert a {FIELD}2˜ merge code (Shift-F9,1,2). The result is shown on the next page.

```
David Robertson
Sullivan, Duffy and Bridge, Attorneys at Law
145 Salmon St.
Portland, OR 97201

Dear Dave,

I am writing to inform you that we will be moving to a new location
on April 1. The address and phone number of our new offices will
be:

Fox & Associates
Medical Malpractice Consultants
1022 SW Vermont St.
Portland, OR 97223
(503) 295-6789

We look forward to continuing our consulting services with
Sullivan, Duffy and Bridge, Attorneys at Law. Please feel free to
contact us at any time during our regular office hours.

Thank you,

                                              Doc 1 Pg 1 Ln 1" Pos 1"
```

Printing Envelopes

We mentioned earlier that you will often use a secondary file with more than one primary file. If you use a name and address secondary file to create form letters, you will probably want to use that same secondary file to print envelopes. To print envelopes, you must create a primary file that defines the size of the envelope and contains the merge-code placeholders for the names and addresses.

If your printer does not have an envelope feed or cannot produce landscape fonts (which print perpendicular to the inserted edge of the envelope), you might not be able to print

Adding the current date

You can add the current date to your form letters by inserting a {DATE} code in the primary file. Follow these steps: **1.** Load the primary file. **2.** With the cursor at the top of the document, press Enter three times to add space, and then press Home,Up Arrow to return the cursor to the top of the document. **3.** Press Shift-F9 (Merge Codes), and select 6 (More). A box appears in the top-right corner of the screen, listing additional merge codes. **4.** Press the Down Arrow key to move the highlight to the {DATE} merge code (or simply type *d*), and then press Enter to insert the code in the primary file. Now every time you merge the primary file, WordPerfect inserts the current date at the top of each document. ♦

Canceling printing

To cancel the printing of the merged documents (or any document): **1.** Press Shift-F7 (Print), and select 4 (Control Printer) and 1 (Cancel Jobs). **2.** Type the number of the print job to be canceled, or type an asterisk (*), and select Y(es) to cancel all print jobs. **3.** Press F7 (Exit) to return to the Editing screen. ♦

envelopes. However, if you follow along, you can check the View Document screen to see what the envelopes look like.

Setting Paper Type, Font Type, and Paper Feed

To print addresses on standard business envelopes (9 1/2 by 4 inches), start by selecting the paper type:

1. Be sure your screen is clear, and then press **Shift-F8** (Format), and select **3** (**D**ocument) and **2** (Initial Codes). WordPerfect displays the Initial Codes screen.

2. Press **Shift-F8** (Format), and select **2** (**P**age) and **7** (Paper **S**ize/Type). This menu appears:

```
Format: Paper Size/Type

                                              Font  Double
Paper type and Orientation    Paper Size   Prompt Loc    Type  Sided  Labels

Envelope - Wide               9.5" x 4"     Yes  Manual  Land  No
Standard                      8.5" x 11"    No   Contin  Port  No
Standard - Wide               11" x 8.5"    No   Contin  Land  No
[ALL OTHERS]                  Width ≤ 8.5"  Yes  Manual        No
```
```
1 Select; 2 Add; 3 Copy; 4 Delete; 5 Edit; N Name Search: 1
```

3. Move the highlight to the Envelope paper type, and select **5** (**E**dit). When the Format: Edit Paper Definition menu appears, be sure that the Paper Size option is 9.5" x 4", that the Paper Type option is Envelope-Wide, and that the Font Type option is Landscape.

4. Select **5** (Location) and **1** (Continuous) to continuously feed envelopes to your printer. The Prompt to Load option automatically changes to No. (If you select Manual, the Prompt to Load option changes to Yes. WordPerfect then sounds a beep when you need to manually feed an envelope into your printer.)

5. Press **F7** (Exit), and with the highlight on the Envelope paper type, select **1** (**S**elect), and then press **F7** (Exit) to return to the Initial Codes screen.

Landscape fonts

Positioning the Address

Next, you need to set margins to position the address in the center of the envelope, like this:

1. With the Initial Codes screen still displayed, press **Shift-F8** (Format), and select **1** (**L**ine) and **7** (**M**argins Left/Right).
2. To print the names and addresses 4 inches from the left margin, type *4*, and press **Enter**. Then type *0* for the right margin, and press **Enter**. To return to the Format menu, press the **Spacebar**.
3. Select **2** (**P**age) and **5** (**M**argins Top/Bottom).
4. Type *0* for the top margin, and press **Enter**. Then type *0* for the bottom margin, and press **Enter**.
5. Press **F7** (Exit) three times to return to the Editing screen.

With the current settings, the address prints too close to the top of the envelope. Fine-tune its position as follows:

1. Press **Shift-F8** (Format), and select **4** (**O**ther) and **1** (**A**dvance).
2. To print the address 2 inches from the top of the envelope, select **3** (**L**ine), type *2*, and press **Enter**.
3. Press **F7** (Exit) to return to the Editing screen.

Inserting the Merge Codes

Now you're ready to insert merge codes into the primary file so that you can merge it with the existing secondary file:

Creating phone lists

You could also use the information from a secondary file, like the one on page 138, to generate a phone list. All you have to do is create a primary file with a field code (Shift-F9,1) for the name field in the secondary file. Then set a tab around the 3-inch or 4-inch position (Shift-F8,1,8), and insert a field code (Shift-F9,1) for the phone number field in the

secondary file. Finally, press Enter to move the cursor just below the first field code, and insert a {PAGE OFF} code (Shift-F9,4) to turn off the hard page breaks that WordPerfect originally inserted in the secondary file. Now, save the new primary file (F7,Y,N), and perform the merge (Ctrl-F9,1). ♦

Mailing labels

When you're ready for more complicated merging techniques, try merging information from a secondary file with a sheet of mailing labels, using WordPerfect's Merge and Labels features. For more information, see "Labels" in the *WordPerfect Reference Manual*. ♦

1. Press **Shift-F9** (Merge/Codes), select **1** (**F**ield), type *1*, press **Enter** to insert a {FIELD}1~ code, and then press **Enter** to start a new line.

2. Repeat the previous step to insert a {FIELD}2~ code and a {FIELD}3~ code into the primary file.

Press **F7** (Exit), save the document as *envelope*, and then clear the screen.

Merging and Printing the Files

Now to test the accuracy of the settings and codes. Merge the primary and secondary files by following these steps:

1. Press **Ctrl-F9** (Merge/Sort), and select **1** (**M**erge).

2. Type *envelope* as the primary file, and press **Enter**. Then type *clients* as the secondary file, and press **Enter**. WordPerfect merges the two files.

3. Press **Home,Home,Up Arrow** to move the cursor to the first "envelope." The other two are visible on your screen, but the hard page breaks ensure that they will print on separate envelopes.

4. Press **Shift-F7** (Print), and select **6** (**V**iew Document) to see how the first envelope will look when it's printed.

5. Press **F7** (Exit) to return to the editing screen, press **F10** (Save), and save the document as *envelope.mrg*.

6. Press **Shift-F7** (Print), and select **1** (**F**ull Document) to print the envelopes.

We printed the envelope shown below with a Hewlett-Packard LaserJet Series II printer.

```
                        David Robertson
                        Sullivan, Duffy and Bridge, Attorneys at Law
                        145 Salmon St.
                        Portland, Or 97201
```

Index

Acknowledgments

Many thanks to Paul Eddington and Kerri Jenson at WordPerfect Corporation; to Michael Monteleone and Kenneth Grey at HandyMAC; and to Steve Lambert, Mary Brande, Bill Teal, and Susan Frankenstein.

About Online Press

Founded in 1986, Online Press is a group of publishing professionals working to make the presentation and access of information manageable, efficient, accurate, and economical. In 1991 we began publishing our popular *Quick Course* computer-book series, offering streamlined instruction for today's busy professional. At Online Press, it is our goal to help computer users quickly learn what they need to know about today's most popular software programs to get their work done efficiently.

Cover design and photography by Tom Draper Design
Interior text design by Joyce Cox and Kjell Swedin
Graphics by Steve Lambert and Pat Kervran
Layout by Kjell Swedin
Printed by Viking Press Inc.
Otabind® cover by Muscle Bound Bindery

Text composition by Online Press in Times Roman, with display type in Helvetica Narrow Bold, using Ventura Publisher and the Linotronic 300 laser imagesetter.

Other *Quick Course* Books

Don't miss the other titles in our *Quick Course* series! Quality books at the unbeatable price of $12.95.

A Quick Course™ in Windows™, Version 3
ISBN 1-879399-00-8 (January 1991)

A Quick Course™ in DOS
ISBN 1-879399-03-2 (June 1991)

A Quick Course™ in Excel 3 for Windows™
ISBN 1-879399-04-0 (August 1991)

A Quick Course™ in Word for Windows™
ISBN 1-879399-05-9 (October 1991)

A Quick Course™ in Lotus® 1-2-3®
ISBN 1-879399-02-4 (December 1991)